PROGRAMMING IN OCCAM™

occam is a trade mark of the INMOS Group of Companies

Prentice-Hall International
Series in Computer Science

C. A. R. Hoare, Series Editor

BACKHOUSE, R. C., *Program Construction and Verification*
BACKHOUSE, R. C., *Syntax of Programming Languages: theory and practice*
de BAKKER, J. W., *Mathematical Theory of Program Correctness*
BJÖRNER, D., and JONES, C. B., *Formal Specification and Software Development*
BORNAT, R., *Programming from First Principles*
CLARK, K. L., and McCABE, F. G., *micro-Prolog: programming in logic*
DROMEY, R. G., *How to Solve it by Computer*
DUNCAN, F., *Microprocessor Programming and Software Development*
ELDER, J., *Construction of Data Processing Software*
GOLDSCHLAGER, L., and LISTER, A., *Computer Science: a modern introduction*
HAYES, I. (Editor), *Specification Case Studies*
HEHNER, E. C. R., *The Logic of Programming*
HENDERSON, P., *Functional Programming: application and implementation*
HOARE, C. A. R., *Communicating Sequential Processes*
HOARE, C. A. R., and SHEPHERDSON, J. A. (Editors), *Mathematical Logic and Programming Languages*
INMOS LTD, *Occam Programming Manual*
JACKSON, M. A., *System Development*
JOHNSTON, H., *Learning to Program*
JONES, C. B., *Systematic Software Development using VDM*
JONES, G., *Programming in occam*
JOSEPH, M., PRASAD, V. R., and NATARAJAN, N., *A Multiprocessor Operating System*
LEW, A., *Computer Science: a mathematical introduction*
MacCALLUM, I., *Pascal for the Apple*
MacCALLUM, I., *UCSD Pascal for the Apple*
PEYTON JONES, S. L., *The Implementation of Functional Programming Languages*
POMBERGER, G., *Software Engineering and Modula-2*
REYNOLDS, J. C., *The Craft of Programming*
SLOMAN, M., and KRAMER, J., *Distributed Systems and Computer Networks*
TENNENT, R. D., *Principles of Programming Languages*
WATT, D. A., WICHMANN, B. A., and FINDLAY, W., *ADA: language and methodology*
WELSH, J., and ELDER, J., *Introduction to Pascal (2nd Edition)*
WELSH, J., ELDER, J., and BUSTARD, D., *Sequential Program Structures*
WELSH, J., and HAY, A., *A Model Implementation of Standard Pascal*
WELSH, J., and McKEAG, M., *Structured System Programming*

PROGRAMMING IN OCCAM™

Geraint Jones

*Programming Research Group,
Oxford University Computing Laboratory*

Prentice-Hall
International

Englewood Cliffs, N.J. London Mexico New Delhi
Rio de Janeiro Singapore Sydney Tokyo Toronto

Library of Congress Cataloging in Publication Data

Jones, Geraint, 1957-
 Programming in occam.
 Includes index.
 1. occam (Computer program language)
 2. Parallel programming (Computer science)
 I. Title.
 QA76.73.02J66   1987   005.13'3   86-30592
 ISBN 0-13-729773-4 (pbk.)

British Library Cataloguing in Publication Data

Jones, Geraint
 Programming in occam. – (Prentice-Hall
 International series in computer science)
 1. occam (Computer program language)
 I. Title
 005.13'3   QA76.73.03
 ISBN 0-13-729773-4

Prentice-Hall Inc., Englewood Cliffs, New Jersey
Prentice-Hall International (UK) Ltd, London
Prentice-Hall of Australia Pty Ltd, Sydney
Prentice-Hall Canada Inc., Toronto
Prentice-Hall Hispanoamericana S.A., Mexico
Prentice-Hall of India Private Ltd, New Delhi
Prentice-Hall of Japan Inc., Tokyo
Prentice-Hall of Southeast Asia Pte Ltd, Singapore
Editora Prentice-Hall do Brasil Ltda, Rio de Janeiro

Printed and bound in Great Britain for
Prentice-Hall International (UK) Ltd,
66 Wood Lane End, Hemel Hempstead, Hertfordshire, HP2 4RG
by A. Wheaton & Co. Ltd, Exeter.

3 4 5   91 90 89 88 87

i nhad, a'm gosododd ar ben y ffordd
heb gael gweld y tiroedd draw

Contents

Preface

This is a book about certain sorts of parallel program. It is certainly not about parallel computers, nor is it really about the *occam* parallel programming language. Hardly any of it is about writing programs to run faster by being executed in parallel.

Long before programmers had made any significant progress with the complexities of programming single processor sequential computers, they knew that the job was only made more complex by trying to get the computer to do two things at once. The parts of an operating system responsible for keeping as many as possible of the peripheral devices in concurrent activity are always the hardest to understand, and the trickiest to get right.

The problems needing solution are rapidly becoming more numerous and difficult. It used to be that the management of concurrency was undertaken on the large scale: creation of new processes, and synchronization and scheduling of their actions were necessarily expensive in comparison to the real work done. These are conditions that seem to persist in the construction of operating systems and of continent-wide communication networks, where processes are consequently long-lived and interact as infrequently as can be contrived. Such are not the conditions experienced by programmers of multi-processor computers, where it becomes feasible to create large numbers of ephemeral processes, and desirable that they communicate frequently.

A great many mechanisms have been suggested for the taming of concurrency, such as semaphores, data monitors, condition queues, critical regions, remote procedure calls and rendezvous, even the disciplined use of shared store. In each case, the aim is to get several processes to co-operate, rather than interfere with each other. The mechanism is to reduce the amount of concurrency in the program by forbidding certain sequences of execution. The essence distilled from these experiments by a number of theoreticians is that the only way to make processes co-operate, usefully to communicate information, is to arrange that their actions be synchronized when they need to interact.

The *occam* language inherits the tradition of theoretical study, being more than reminiscent of recent work on the mathematics of synchronization. It is intended by its devisers as the 'assembly code' of the INMOS transputer, a microprocessor designed to be used in relatively large numbers to make a single machine, yet capable of managing a large number of concurrent tasks within the one processor. The programmer is therefore encouraged to think of process creation, and of synchronization and scheduling operations, as being as cheap as any other 'primitive' actions. Even on a conventional processor, neither process creation nor scheduling need be any more expensive than, say, procedure invocation. This startling scale of costs gives the programmer much greater freedom of expression, and leads to an unaccustomed programming style. If you think that this book is about anything, I would prefer that you think it is about this style.

The book begins with an introduction to *occam* sufficient to make the rest of the work intelligible to anyone who is already able to write and understand sequential programs. Some *occam* idioms are exercised to help to give you an understanding of the way the language can be used. The bulk of the text is devoted to a number of sizeable examples; these are programs written to give me material to discuss in teaching the use of *occam*.

At the back of the book you will find a concise summary of the *occam* language, drawn from material in the *Programming Manual*, published in this same series. Finally, there are reproduced the complete codes of the larger examples. I do not expect that anyone might want to read hundreds of lines of code, but their presence may make it easier to settle ambiguities in the presentation in the text.

*　　　*　　　*

Several people will be content to believe that they encouraged me to put this material between covers, some of them did, for which I am duly grateful, but I would not dream of burdening anyone else with a suspicion of the responsibility for such inadequacies as remain.

1 An introduction to occam

As far as will concern us here, an *occam* program is simply a process, which may have some free identifiers that have specific meanings dependent on the computer on which the program is to be run. A process describes some actions that are to be performed: that is, it is the expression of an algorithm. Each process may be either a primitive process, or a composite process consisting of a number of definitions and simpler component processes bound together by process constructors. The structure of constructed processes is indicated by a fixed layout of the source text, with each component appearing on a new line, slightly indented from the keyword that introduced the whole construction.

Processes that do nothing

The simplest of the primitive processes is SKIP, which is the process that does nothing at all. In many programming languages, you are obliged to write nothing (that is, not to write anything at all) if you want 'nothing' done; you will see later that SKIP serves as useful a purpose in *occam* as that of zero in the decimal notation for numbers.

The process STOP also does 'nothing', but unlike SKIP it fails to terminate. You can think of it as being what happens when something goes wrong, like a deadlock, or some illegal machine operation. Nothing can happen in a sequential process after it has stopped, but things can happen in parallel with a stopped process. You might not expect to write the STOP process very often in your programs, but it is the rational thing to do when something unexpected happens, because it ensures that the part of a network of processes that has failed is brought to a standstill without affecting other processes, at least until they come to depend on the broken part.

It is also useful to have STOP around so as to be able to describe the effect of compound processes that 'go wrong', for example by becoming deadlocked. A process is said to be deadlocked if there is nothing which it is able to do next, but it has not finished properly. A parallel program which becomes deadlocked typically does so because each of its processes is waiting for one of the others to do something.

Sequential processes

In programs which execute sequentially, the work is done by assigning values to variables, and subsequently basing decisions on the values of those variables. The *occam* assignment has the form

```
variable := expression
```

Each expression has a value, as explained later, which is just a bit pattern of the size of a 'word' on your computer, and every variable is capable of storing a word sized bit pattern. Of course, there are operators which treat these bit patterns as if they represented numbers, or truth values, or characters, but no type distinction is enforced by the language or its compilers.

A sequence of operations is described by writing them one under the other, under and slightly indented from the keyword SEQ. The sequence executes by executing each of its components in the order in which they are written. Of course, if there are no components at all, then the sequence does nothing, and behaves just like SKIP. Thus

```
SEQ
  x := 3
  y := x + 7
  x := x + 6
  z := x + 1
  x := (y + z) / 2
```

has the overall effect of setting each of the variables x, y, z to 10, albeit in a somewhat perverse way: first x is set to three, then y to seven more than x, then x is changed to nine, z is set to one more than it, and finally x is set to the average of y and z, which is of course also ten.

Decisions based on the values of variables are made by a conditional process. This construction consists of the keyword IF written above a list of components, each slightly indented. Each component is either another conditional nested within the first, or consists of an expression (the condition) and, below the condition and a little further indented, a process. The whole conditional executes by looking down the list of components, and the components of nested conditionals, until a condition is found whose value is TRUE. If one is found then the corresponding process and only that process is executed, and the whole conditional terminates. It is an error for no condition to evaluate to TRUE, for example if there are no components, so in that case the conditional stops.

```
IF
   n < 0
     sign := -1
   n = 0
     sign := 0
   n > 0
     sign := 1
```

sets the value of the variable *sign* to one of minus one, zero, or plus one, according as the variable *n* has a negative, zero, or positive value.

Since it is defined that the textually first of the processes corresponding to a TRUE condition is selected, the process

```
IF
   n = 0
     sign := 0
   n <= 0
     sign := -1
   TRUE
     sign := 1
```

describes exactly the same effect as the former, but is much less clear. In general, it is good style to use constraints that describe as precisely as is convenient the conditions under which a process is to be executed.

Parallel processes

Just as a list of actions can be described as happening in a strict sequence, so in *occam* it is possible to specify that each of a list of actions is to happen, without specifying an order in which they must happen. Such a parallel composition is indicated by writing the actions one under the other, under and slightly indented from the

keyword PAR. The parallel composition executes by executing each
of its components, until each has terminated. Of course, if there
are no components, the effect is the same as SKIP, and if any of the
components fails to terminate, for example by stopping, then the
composition cannot terminate.

```
PAR
  x := y - 1
  z := y + 1
```

sets the values of x and z to be one less than, and one more than,
respectively, the value of y. There is, however, no guarantee that the
assignments will not happen in the other order, or at precisely the
same moment. Because of this, for a parallel composition to be legal,
none of its components may change any variable which is used in any
of the other branches: it would be wrong, for example, to try to write

```
PAR
  x := y - 1
  z := x + 2
```

because x is used in the second component, but changed in the first
component.

If such mutual interference is not allowed, how then are concurrent processes to communicate? The answer is that they do so by
input and output over channels. The output process

```
channel ! expression
```

sends the value of the expression over the channel. Similarly, the
input process

```
channel ? variable
```

receives a value from the channel and stores it in the variable. Each
of these communications waits for the other, so that an output does
not happen until the corresponding input happens, and vice versa.

There is an abbreviation which is useful when complex data are
to be transmitted, for example where many streams of data are multiplexed along one channel, and some identification must be sent with
each item. A sequence of inputs (or of outputs) along one channel
may be written as a single primitive process, separating the target
variables (or expressions) by semicolons

```
channel ? variable.1; variable.2; ... variable.n
```

This has precisely the same meaning as

```
SEQ
  channel ? variable.1
  channel ? variable.2
         .
         .
         .
  channel ? variable.n
```

In combination, an input and an output behave just like an assignment, except that the expression and variable are in different, concurrently executing processes. In particular, the assignment

```
variable := expression
```

is exactly the same as

```
PAR
  channel ! expression
  channel ? variable
```

provided that it is legal to write the latter in the particular context. Just as there are rules about the use of variables in concurrently executing processes, so also each end (the input end, or the output end) of a channel may be used in only one of the components of a PAR construction.

Decisions may also be distributed across several processes, using an alternative, which is similar to a conditional except in that the choice can depend on whether another process is performing an output. An alternative is written with the keyword ALT above a list of components, each of which is either an alternative, or consists of a guard with below that a process which is indented a little further. A guard may be an input process, or SKIP, or either of these simple guards preceded by an expression and an ampersand sign, as for example

```
ALT
  red.selected & red ? x
    out ! x
  green.selected & green ? x
    out ! x
  NOT (red.selected OR green.selected) & SKIP
    out ! default.value
```

An alternative waits until there is a guard which is 'ready'. An input guard becomes ready when a corresponding output is possible; a SKIP guard is always ready; and a guard preceded by an expression can only become ready if both the value of the expression is TRUE, and the process part of the guard is ready. When some guard has become ready, one of the ready guards is selected and executed, followed by the corresponding process. After this the alternative terminates. At most one of the branches of an alternative is selected; if no guard ever becomes ready (for example, if there are no components in the alternative) then the whole alternative is deadlocked, like STOP.

The example alternative above will accept an input from either the *red* or the *green* channel, provided that the value of the corresponding variable, *red.selected* or *green.selected*, is TRUE, and having accepted that input into the variable *x*, it then re-outputs the value down the channel *out*. In case neither variable is TRUE, only the third guard is ready, so the alternative sends the *default.value* and then terminates.

Data declarations

Each name used in an *occam* program must be declared before it can be used. There are declarations which allow you to give names to constant values, to variables, and to channels.

Constant definitions do not introduce any new objects into the program, they serve merely to give names to particular values. They are written with the keyword DEF followed by some definitions of the form

```
name = constant.expression
```

each definition separated from the next by a comma, and with a colon at the end. The effect is to allow you to use the *name* in the process that follows, wherever you want to refer to the value of the *constant.expression*. As an example, the declarations

```
DEF red = 0, red.and.amber = 1, green = 2, amber = 3 :
DEF first.state = red, last.state = amber :
```

might appear in a traffic light controller. It would then be possible to test, for example, whether

```
current.state = last.state
```

rather than comparing *current.state* for equality with 3, which would be altogether more obscure.

Variables, as has already been indicated, are capable of storing bit patterns of some fixed size. They are declared by listing their names after the keyword VAR, above the process that will use them. The names are separated by commas, and there is a colon at the end of the list. The traffic light controller might well include, for example,

```
VAR current.state, queue.size :
```

Initially, a variable has no defined value, but once it has been set by an assignment or an input, its value is the last value that was stored into it. The usual place to find variable declarations is accordingly just before the keyword SEQ. Components of a sequence communicate with each other by one component leaving a value in a variable, and a later component reading that value. The traffic light controller might begin

```
DEF first.state = red, last.state = amber :
VAR current.state, queue.size :
SEQ
   current.state := first.state
   queue.size := 0
      ⋮
```

Channels are declared in the same way as variables, except that the keyword is CHAN. Somewhere within the scope of each channel declaration there will be two concurrent processes, one of which sends output to the channel, the other of which takes input from it. It is therefore usual to find channel declarations immediately in front of PAR constructions.

Arrays

There is only one device for structuring data in *occam*: you may make one-dimensional arrays of constants, variables or channels. An array of variables is declared by giving a constant expression in brackets after the name.

```
name[count]
```

This indicates that a number, equal to the value of the *count*, of variables are to be declared, which can be referred to by indexing the name of the array with expressions whose values range from zero up to *count* − 1. For example, in the scope of the definition

```
VAR a[137]  :
```

there are declared 137 variables, called $a[0]$, $a[1]$, $a[2]$, ..., $a[136]$, each variable independent of the others. Arrays of channels are similar.

An array of constants is called a table, and is denoted by an expression of the form

```
TABLE[expression.zero, expression.one,
                     expression.two, ... , expression.n]
```

(This is an example of a broken line: long lines of *occam* can be can be split in places where it is obvious that they are not yet complete, so long as the second part of the line does not start to the left of the first part. Be warned that the rules will probably not agree with you about which are the places at which a line is obviously incomplete!)

Table expressions can be used in DEF declarations, or can appear to the left of an index, so that the value of

```
TABLE[expression.zero, expression.one,
                     expression.two, ... ][2]
```

is the same as the value of *expression.two*, for example.

In case the values of the components are always going to be in the range zero to 255, as for example when the values represent characters, *occam* allows you to specify that the values are to be packed one to a byte in the store of the machine. An array of byte variables is declared by adding the keyword BYTE after the opening bracket of the declarations; a byte table is denoted by including the keyword BYTE after the opening bracket of the denotation. A byte array of constants or variables is indexed by putting the keyword BYTE after the opening bracket of the index. For the present, the only reason for being concerned with byte arrays is that *occam* has a convenient denotation for byte arrays of characters: a string, which is written as a sequence of characters enclosed in double quotes,

```
"This is a string"
```

is a byte array, the first (zeroth) byte of which contains the length, and the subsequent bytes contain the characters in sequence. This string represents the same array of constants as does

```
TABLE[BYTE 16, 'T', 'h', 'i', 's','*s', 'i', 's','*s',
                 'a','*s', 's', 't', 'r', 'i', 'n', 'g']
```

A character between single quotes denotes a constant bit-pattern just like any other, corresponding to the ASCII code for that character, and the sequence '*s' represents the space character, that is 32. I could have written this as a space between quotes, ' ', but the asterisk form is clearer. There are asterisk-sequences for space (*s), carriage-return (*c), the newline character (*n), the quote characters (*' and *"), and of course for asterisk (**), which can be used either in character (single) quotes, or as elements of a string. In the scope of the declaration

```
DEF s = "This*sis*sa*sstring" :
```

(which is yet again the same byte array as before) the value of s[BYTE 0] is 16, and the value of s[BYTE 16] is 103, which is the ASCII code of the character '*g*'.

Process declarations

Names may be given to whole processes by means of PROC declarations. These are introduced by a line of the form

```
PROC name =
```

which is followed by the process to be called *name*, indented slightly, and terminated by a colon. The effect is that anywhere in the process that follows the declaration you can write *name* to mean the whole of the named process. (That means the named process is not in the scope of the declaration, so it is not possible to invoke it from within itself.)

A named process may have a list of formal parameters included after its name in the declaration. The nature of each parameter is indicated by one of the keywords VALUE, VAR, or CHAN, meaning a value (run-time constant), variable, or channel. You may omit the keyword in front of a second or subsequent parameter of a particular kind. Arrays are indicated by writing an empty pair of brackets after the name of the array.

The process is invoked by putting a corresponding list of actual parameters after the name at the point of call. The effect is the same as if the body of the named process had been written in place of the call, but with the actual parameters substituted for the formal parameters. Thus, for example

```
PROC assign.character(VAR x, VALUE s[], i) =
  x := s[BYTE i]          :

VAR ch :
SEQ
  assign.character(ch, "This is a string", 13)
       :
       :
```

has the effect of assigning the code of '*r*', that is the 13th character of the string, to the variable *ch*, exactly as though the program had been written

```
VAR ch :
SEQ
  ch := "This is a string" [13]
       :
       :
```

Loops and arrays of processes

There are two kinds of loops in *occam*: unbounded WHILE loops, and indexed, bounded FOR loops. Unbounded loops are necessarily sequential in *occam*, but there are many forms of FOR loop representing different sorts of regular activity.

An unbounded loop is written with the keyword WHILE, followed by an expression (the condition), with a process (the body) below and slightly indented from it. It executes by testing the value of the condition and then, provided that its value is TRUE, executing the body. When the body has terminated, the condition is re-tested, so that the body is executed a number of times, in sequence, for as long as the condition remains TRUE. The whole WHILE loop terminates when the condition is tested and found to be FALSE.

```
SEQ
  x := 0
  v[n] := key
  WHILE  v[x] <> key
    x := x + 1
```

sets *x* to be the index of the first variable in the array *v* which contains the value *key*, by first posting a sentinel at *v*[*n*]. ('<>' is the *occam* notation for 'not equal'.)

A bounded loop may be thought of as being an array of processes. Loops can be made from each of the ALT, IF, PAR and SEQ constructions, by putting a replicator of the form

```
name = [base FOR count]
```

after the keyword, and then writing a single component (of the kind appropriate to the construction) below and slightly indented from the keyword. The *base* and *count* are expressions, and the meaning of such a FOR loop is the same as that of a construction formed from the same keyword followed by *count* copies of the component with the name taking on the values *base*, *base* + 1, ..., *base* + *count* − 1 in successive copies.

A FOR loop stands for a repetition of the constructor with which it is made. In the same way that

$$\prod_{year=1280}^{1341} entity_{year}$$

stands for the multiplication of sixty-two values,

$$entity_{1280} \times entity_{1281} \times \ldots \times entity_{1341}$$

so too the SEQ-FOR loop

```
SEQ year = [1280 FOR 62]
   celebrate.Christmas(year)
```

stands for the sequential composition of sixty-two processes

```
SEQ
   celebrate.Christmas(1280)
   celebrate.Christmas(1281)
           ⋮
   celebrate.Christmas(1341)
```

Thus, SEQ-FOR loops are just like FOR loops in languages like ALGOL or PASCAL; but that you may not assign to the loop index, and it is not declared outside the body of the loop.

The bodies of parallel PAR-FOR loops are executed concurrently, so such loops behave like arrays of parallel processes. A conditional loop, written with IF and FOR, performs a bounded search, so

```
SEQ
  v[n] := key
  IF i = [0 FOR n + 1]
    v[i] = key
      x := i
```

has precisely the same effect as that of the WHILE loop above. The same search can be done, without the use of a sentinel, by writing

```
DEF otherwise = TRUE, not.found = n :
IF
  IF i = [0 FOR n]
    v[i] = key
      x := i
  otherwise
    x := not.found
```

Here, *x* is set to *not.found* precisely when there is no occurrence of the value *key* in the array. You should now see the reason for allowing conditionals as components of conditionals, and alternatives as components of alternatives!

Some dialects of *occam* allow you to construct FOR loops not only from constructed processes, but also from the primitive assignments, inputs and outputs. An expression like

```
name [base FOR count]
```

is called a slice, and denotes all of the variables (or values)

```
name[base], name[base+1], ..., name[base+count-1]
```

Slices may be assigned

```
dest[dest.base FOR count]:=srce[srce.base FOR count]
```

or they may be communicated

```
PAR
  channel ? dest[dest.base FOR count]
  channel ! srce[srce.base FOR count]
```

In each case, both of the slices concerned must be of the same size, and the effect is to set each of the *count* variables in *dest*, from *dest[dest.base]* upwards, to the values of the *count* variables in *srce*, again, counting from *srce[srce.base]* upwards. Do not confuse slice communications with the semicolon abbreviation for a sequence of communications: single slice operations must match with other slice operations; the semicolon denotes a sequence of unrelated communications.

There are also byte slices which are denoted by

```
name [BYTE base FOR count]
```

and which may be assigned or communicated into other byte slices.

Expressions

Every simple expression in *occam* denotes a bit pattern the size of the word on the computer that is executing the program. There is no defined precedence between the various operators, so parentheses are generally needed to disambiguate an expression with more than one operator. The only exception to this rule is that associative operators do not need parentheses. All expressions are built of operators, constants, variables, and indexed arrays, so that evaluating an expression cannot possibly have a side-effect.

A number of operators are best understood by regarding each bit pattern as the twos complement representation of an integer: the values of

```
a + b        a - b        a * b        a / b        a \ b
```

are the sum, difference, product, quotient and remainder of a and b. The result of a division is an integer, rounded towards zero, and the remainder is given by

```
(a \ b)      =       (a - (b * (a / b)))
```

provided b is not zero.

The usual six relational operators:

```
a < b    a <= b    a = b    a >= b    a > b    a <> b
```

compare their operands as though they represented signed integers, and return one of the values TRUE or FALSE. There is one other relational operator intended for comparing the values of a clock which counts cyclically through all possible word sized bit-patterns: the expression

```
a AFTER b
```

is TRUE or FALSE according as a would be reached sooner by successively incrementing b, ignoring overflow, than by decrementing it.
(Almost half of all bit patterns are AFTER any given bit-pattern.)

Expressions made up with the following operators have Boolean
values.

NOT a

is TRUE when a is FALSE and FALSE when a is TRUE. Provided that each
of a and b is either TRUE or FALSE, the values of

```
a AND b          a OR b          a >< b
```

are TRUE if both of a and b are TRUE, if either one is TRUE, or if exactly
one is TRUE, repectively; they are FALSE otherwise. The AND and OR
operators evaluate their left argument first, and then the right argument only should it be needed to decide the result. This means that,
for example, bounds checks should precede array accesses

```
(0 <= i) AND (i < size) AND (a[i] = x)
```

The effects of some operators are most easily described by thinking of the operands as bit patterns. The values of

```
a \/ b           a /\ b           a >< b
```

are the bit by bit 'logical or', 'logical and', and 'exclusive or' of the
patterns a and b.

NOT a

is the bit by bit (ones) complement of a.

Since the values TRUE and FALSE are, respectively, a word of one-
bits and a word of zero-bits

```
(x /\ TRUE)  =   x
(x /\ FALSE) =   0
(x \/ 0)     =   x
```

This means that you can write conditional expressions, such as

```
(a /\ (p < q)) \/ (b /\ (p = q)) \/ (c /\ (p > q))
```

the value of which is one of a, b, or c according as p is less than, equal
to, or greater than q.

The shift operators displace a pattern a by b number of bits, so
that this many bits are lost from one end of the pattern, and the same

number of zero bits are shifted in at the other end of the pattern. The values of

```
a << b        a >> b
```

are the same as the pattern *a* but shifted left and right respectively by *b* bit positions.

There is nothing to stop you constructing bit patterns by bit manipulation, and then treating these patterns as twos complement integers. Provided that *logarithm* is less than the number of bits in a word, the value of

```
1 << logarithm
```

is a word with only the *logarithm*[th] bit set, that is $2^{logarithm}$. The value of

```
(NOT 0) >> 1
```

is a word of one bits, excepting that the most significant bit, that is the sign bit, is zero; this value is therefore the largest positive integer in the range that can be represented on your particular machine, written in a way that is independent of the word length of the machine.

```
NOT ((NOT 0) >> 1)
```

is similarly a word of zero bits, excepting for a one in the sign bit, so is the most negative integer that can be represented. Another construction which I will use later is

```
NOT ((NOT 0) << logarithm)
```

which is the bit pattern in which the least significant *logarithm* number of bits are set. This is useful for making masks, so that, for example, in the scope of

```
DEF control = NOT ((NOT 0) << 5) :
```

the value of

```
control /\ 'G'
```

is seven, which is the character code known as 'control-and-G'.

2   Programming structures

In the next few pages, the various pipes and joints of *occam* are demonstrated in some small plumbing exercises. Although these examples may seem unrealistic or overly elaborate for their size, they are intended to show some practical programming techniques.

Simple sequential processes

It is almost traditional that the first program anyone writes in a new programming language is one that writes "Hello", or some equally imaginative greeting, to the screen of their terminal. In an *occam* environment, the terminal screen is likely to be accessible as a channel: values output to the channel being displayed on the screen as characters. A first, unexciting attempt at the "Hello" program is

```
SEQ
   terminal.screen ! 'H'
   terminal.screen ! 'e'
   terminal.screen ! 'l'
   terminal.screen ! 'l'
   terminal.screen ! 'o'
```

or more compactly

```
terminal.screen !  ! 'H'; 'e'; 'l'; 'l'; 'o'
```

Looking for ways to generalize the program, it would be natural to write a loop that outputs each of the characters of an *occam* string. Recall that a string is a BYTE array, with the number of characters being string[BYTE 0] so that a program to write string should behave like

16

```
SEQ
  output ! string[BYTE 1]
  output ! string[BYTE 2]
         :
  output ! string[BYTE string[BYTE 0]]
```

This is patently a candidate for a SEQ-FOR loop, which can be written

```
SEQ character.number = [1 FOR string[BYTE 0]]
  output ! string[BYTE character.number]
```

The process can be packaged as a named process, corresponding to a procedure in a language such as PASCAL, for writing the characters of a string to a channel

```
PROC write.string(CHAN output, VALUE string[]) =
  -- Send the characters of the string along output
  SEQ character.number = [1 FOR string[BYTE 0]]
    output ! string[BYTE character.number]          :
```

The line with the hyphens on it is a comment: these can appear at the end of any line in an *occam* program, even otherwise blank ones as here. Writing comments summarizing the behaviour of named processes is probably a good habit to cultivate.

In consequence of some unfortunate experiences in my past, I have come to expect my computer to greet me with the shibboleth "Bootifrolo". This might be done by using *write.string*, as follows

```
PROC write.string(CHAN output, VALUE string[]) =
  -- Send the characters of the string along output
  SEQ character.number = [1 FOR string[BYTE 0]]
    output ! string[BYTE character.number]          :

write.string(terminal.screen, "Bootifrolo")
```

Simple parallel processes

The simplest thing that you can usefully want a process to be doing, at the same time as another process is doing something else, is to copy data from one channel to another. This is just a matter of repeatedly taking input from one channel, storing it in a local variable, and then sending the value of the variable along another channel.

```
VAR local :
SEQ
  source ? local
  sink ! local
```

Why you might possibly want this done should be apparent: the local variable acts as a buffer in the data stream passing along the two channels. This copying process can be packaged as a named process that can be used to buffer any unbounded data stream passing between two processes

```
PROC buffer(CHAN source, sink) =
  WHILE TRUE
    VAR local :
    SEQ
      source ? local
      sink ! local                :
```

Now whereas the producer and the consumer process are tightly synchronized in a program like

```
PROC producer(CHAN output.stream) =
  WHILE TRUE
    VAR datum :
    SEQ
      ... calculate a new datum
      output.stream ! datum              :

PROC consumer(CHAN input.stream) =
  WHILE TRUE
    VAR datum :
    SEQ
      input.stream ? datum
      ... calculate using the datum    :

CHAN data.stream :
PAR
  producer(data.stream)
  consumer(data.stream)
```

with neither able to get ahead of the other, by adding a buffer

```
CHAN data.from.producer, data.to.consumer :
PAR
  producer(data.from.producer)
  buffer(data.from.producer, data.to.consumer)
  consumer(data.to.consumer)
```

the two are slightly decoupled. The producer is now able to run up to one item of data ahead of the consumer. ('Magic buffers', so called, that would allow the consumer to run an item ahead of the producer are a mite more difficult to implement, even in *occam*!)

More buffering is easily provided by inserting more buffers in the data path. This is like a 'fall-through' first-in-first-out store, where each item of data is passed along a register until it reaches the last unoccupied location. Several items can be in independent 'free fall' at once if the buffer is fairly empty.

```
CHAN data.stream[number.of.buffers + 1] :
PAR
  producer(data.stream[0])
  PAR index = [0 FOR number.of.buffers]
    buffer(data.stream[index], data.stream[index + 1])
  consumer(data.stream[number.of.buffers])
```

There is, of course, nothing to stop you programming a buffer with an array of variables governed by one process, just as in any conventional programming language.

Synchronization by control signals

You might try putting the buffer process into the stream that goes to the terminal screen from the "Bootifrolo" program

```
CHAN internal.stream :
PAR
  write.string(internal.stream, "Bootifrolo")
  buffer(internal.stream, terminal.screen)
```

but this is not quite right. The *buffer* initially performs well, and copies all of the characters to the screen. Eventually, however, all of the string has been sent, and the *write.string* process terminates. This leaves the *buffer* in a somewhat undignified state, trying to perform an input on *internal.stream* when there will never again be a corresponding output. The program is deadlocked.

Some way is needed of telling the buffer that it should not expect any more input along its *source* channel, and that it should accordingly terminate. The process

```
PROC copy.characters(CHAN source, end.of.source, sink)=
  -- Copy characters from source to sink
  -- until there is a signal on end.of.source
  VAR more.characters.expected :
  SEQ
    more.characters.expected := TRUE
    WHILE more.characters.expected
      VAR ch :
      ALT
        source ? ch
          sink ! ch
        end.of.source ? ANY
          more.characters.expected := FALSE    :
```

behaves just like the *buffer*, copying from *source* to *sink*, except that it may also take input from the channel *end.of.source*. The keyword ANY just means that the actual value received is immaterial, so it need not be stored in a variable. When an input signal is received on *end.of.source*, the variable *more.characters.expected* is set FALSE, so the WHILE loop terminates.

The right way of buffering the output of *write.string* is to send its output to a *copy.characters* process, and to send a termination signal after the whole string has been sent. Since the value received as a termination signal is ignored, it does not matter what is sent: outputting ANY has the effect of sending something unspecified.

```
CHAN internal.stream, end.of.internal.stream :
PAR
  SEQ
    write.string(internal.stream, "Bootifrolo")
    end.of.internal.stream ! ANY
  copy.characters(internal.stream,
                  end.of.internal.stream,
                  terminal.screen)
```

In the case of the *copy.characters* process, there is no need to use a signal on an extra channel, because there is already a channel going in the right direction. The data and the termination signal can be multiplexed onto one channel. You could select some value, say

```
DEF end.of.stream = -1
```

which is not a possible character value, and send that after the last
real character of the message

```
DEF end.of.stream = -1 :
CHAN internal.stream :
PAR

  PROC write.string(CHAN output, VALUE string[]) =
    -- Send the characters of the string along output
    SEQ character.number = [1 FOR string[BYTE 0]]
      output ! string[BYTE character.number]          :
  SEQ
    write.string(internal.stream, "Bootifrolo")
    internal.stream ! end.of.stream

  PROC copy.characters(CHAN source, sink) =
    -- Copy characters from source to sink
    -- until a signal arrives on end.of.stream
    VAR more.characters.expected :
    SEQ
      more.characters.expected := TRUE
      WHILE more.characters.expected
        VAR ch :
        SEQ
          source ? ch
          IF
            ch <> end.of.stream
              sink ! ch
            ch = end.of.stream
              more.characters.expected := FALSE   :

  copy.characters(internal.stream, terminal.screen)
```

In this particular case, there is little to choose between the two styles:
the latter program may be marginally more efficient.

In many cases there will be no data-stream going in the right
direction, and a channel exclusively for synchronization will be es-
sential. A circular buffer implemented using an array of variables is
an example of this kind. Assume that the array is declared by

```
VAR datum[size] :
```

and that the variables

```
VAR reader, writer :
```

have values in the range zero to *size* − 1, so that the oldest value to leave the buffer will be found at *datum*[*reader*], and the next to enter the buffer will be written to *datum*[*writer*]. It will be convenient to keep track of the number of unoccupied locations in the buffer by a further variable

```
VAR count :
```

whose value ranges from zero, for a full buffer, to *size* for an empty one.

There are two activities in which the buffer must be able to participate: provided that it is not full, that is that *count* > 0, it must be possible to add another value to the buffer

```
SEQ
   source ? datum[writer]
   writer := (writer + 1) \ size
   count  := count - 1
```

and provided that *count* < *size* it must be possible for the oldest value to be read from the buffer

```
SEQ
   sink ! datum[reader]
   reader := (reader + 1) \ size
   count  := count + 1
```

The buffer must allow the producing and consuming processes to control its activity, selecting between writing and reading, provided only that there is room to write, or something to read, respectively.

Arbitration like this requires an ALT process, with the reading and writing actions being guarded by the conditions under which they may happen—*count* > 0 and *count* < *size*—and the readiness of the consumer and the producer. Since the consumer is ready when the buffer can output to *sink* and the producer when the buffer can input from *source* it is tempting to write

```
ALT
  count > 0   &   source ? datum[writer]
    SEQ
      writer := (writer + 1) \ size
      count  := count - 1
  count < size   &   sink ! datum[reader]
    SEQ
      reader := (reader + 1) \ size
      count  := count + 1
```

but output processes cannot be used to guard alternatives. The solution is to have a control signal from the consuming process indicating that it is ready to accept an input from *sink*. There is no need for the corresponding request before a write to the buffer, because the input along *source* serves perfectly well in place of a control signal.

```
PROC circular.buffer(CHAN source, request, sink) =

  -- Copy from source to sink, buffering up to size
  -- items. A signal is required on request before
  -- each item is read from sink.

  VAR reader, writer, count, datum[size] :
  SEQ
    reader := 0
    writer := 0
    count  := size
    WHILE TRUE
      ALT
        count > 0   &   source ? datum[writer]
          SEQ
            writer := (writer + 1) \ size
            count  := count - 1
        count < size   &   request ? ANY
          SEQ
            sink ! datum[reader]
            reader := (reader + 1) \ size
            count  := count + 1                    :
```

It is the responsibility of the consumer, whenever it reads from the buffer, to precede the input from *source* by an output on *request*, performing two communications in sequence

```
SEQ
  request ! ANY
  source ? ...
```

The ultimate consumer can be relieved of this burden at the expense
of an extra process, executing concurrently with the circular buffer

```
PROC multiple.buffer(CHAN source, sink) =
  -- Copy from source to sink,
  -- buffering up to size+1 items.
  CHAN request, data :
  PAR
    circular.buffer(source, request, data)

    WHILE TRUE
      VAR datum :
      SEQ
        request ! ANY
        data ? datum
        sink ! datum                        :
```

The resulting *multiple.buffer* process has a behaviour which is in-
distinguishable from that of a chain of *size* + 1 single-item *buffer*
processes acting in parallel.

Processes that evaluate expressions

Suppose now that you have a need to calculate the parity of the
characters that are being sent to the terminal. (The parity of a
character is an indication of whether there is an even or an odd
number of one-bits in the binary representation of its code.)

In a language like PASCAL, you might write a function to calculate
the parity of a character which was given to it as a parameter, but
in *occam* (there being no 'function's) the natural construction is a
named process

```
PROC calculate.parity(VALUE ch, VAR parity) =
  ... Return the parity of ch in parity
```

which returns the result by way of a VAR parameter. A representation
will be necessary for parity values: I will choose the truth values

```
DEF even = TRUE, odd = NOT even :
```

although it turns out that the process will be independent of the particular bit pattern chosen to represent *even*.

Calculating the parity of *ch* involves considering each bit of *ch*: the simplest thing to do is to take them one at a time in sequence. (Expert bit twiddlers may care to code an algorithm logarithmic in the number of bits in the character.) The expression

```
ch /\ (1 << bit.number)
```

is either zero or not according as the $bit.number^{th}$ bit of *ch*, counting from zero at the least significant end. The loop

```
SEQ bit.number = [0 FOR number.of.bits.in.character]
  IF
    (ch /\ (1 << bit.number)) = 0
      SKIP
    (ch /\ (1 << bit.number)) <> 0
      parity := NOT parity
```

complements the value of *parity* as often as there are one bits in *ch*.

Since exclusive-or behaves like a conditional complement operation, the conditional process in the middle of this loop can be abbreviated to a simple assignment

```
parity := parity >< ((ch /\ (1 << bit.number)) <> 0)
```

with the same effect.

If *parity* is initialized to *even*, then its final value indicates the parity of *ch*, implementing the named process *calculate.parity*

```
DEF even = TRUE, odd = NOT even :

PROC calculate.parity(VALUE ch, VAR parity) =
  -- Return the parity of ch in parity
  DEF number.of.bits.in.character = 8 :
  SEQ
    parity := even
    SEQ bit.number=[0 FOR number.of.bits.in.character]
      parity := parity ><
                    ((ch /\ (1 << bit.number)) <> 0) :
```

Using parallelism as a tool for program modularity

If for some reason you wanted to modify the *write.string* process
so that it wrote only the even parity characters from its argument,
ignoring the rest, you could write

```
PROC write.even.parity.string(CHAN output,
                                  VALUE string[]) =
  SEQ character.number = [1 FOR string[BYTE 0]]
    VAR parity :
    SEQ
      calculate.parity(string[BYTE character.number],
                                                  parity)
      IF
        parity = even
          output ! string[BYTE character.number]
        parity = odd
          SKIP                                              :
```

This process is specialized: it performs its task well enough, but there
are no recognizable separate components performing subtasks, which
you might be able to use again in other programs. The code for
selecting characters according to their parity is mixed in with the
code for turning a string into a sequence of output processes.

A more modular program might use a process which turns a
string into a sequence of outputs

```
PROC write.string(CHAN output, VALUE string[]) =
... Send the characters of string along output
```

and a separate process which splits a stream of characters into two
streams according to their parities

```
PROC divide.on.parity(CHAN source, end.of.source,
                               even.sink, odd.sink) =
... Copy the even parity characters from source to
... even.sink, odd parity to odd.sink, until a signal
... arrives on end.of.source
```

This latter process can be used to filter out the odd or even
parity character codes from any data stream.

```
PROC divide.on.parity(CHAN source, end.of.source,
                                   even.sink, odd.sink) =
  -- Copy the even parity characters from source to
  -- even.sink, odd parity to odd.sink, until a signal
  -- arrives on end.of.source
  VAR more.characters.expected :
  SEQ
    more.characters.expected := TRUE
    WHILE more.characters.expected
      VAR ch :
      ALT
        source ? ch
          VAR parity :
          SEQ
            calculate.parity(ch, parity)
            IF
              parity = even
                even.sink ! ch
              parity = odd
                odd.sink ! ch
        end.of.source ? ANY
          more.characters.expected := FALSE              :
```

Since only the even parity stream is wanted in the present application, the unwanted stream must be discarded

```
PROC consume(CHAN source, end.of.source) =
  -- Discard input from source until a signal
  -- arrives on end.of.source
  VAR more.characters.expected :
  SEQ
    more.characters.expected := TRUE
    WHILE more.characters.expected
      ALT
        source ? ANY
          SKIP
        end.of.source ? ANY
          more.characters.expected := FALSE    :
```

Using the *divide.on.parity* component my "Bootifrolo" program might be written

```
PROC write.string(CHAN output, VALUE string[]) =
... Send the characters of string along output

PROC divide.on.parity(CHAN source, end.of.source,
                            even.sink, odd.sink) =
... Copy from source to even.sink or odd.sink

PROC consume(CHAN source, end.of.source) =
... Discard from source, until end.of.source

CHAN both.parities, end.of.both,
     odd.parity, end.of.odd.parity :
PAR
  SEQ
    write.string(both.parities, "Booting from Floppy")
    end.of.both ! ANY

  SEQ
    divide.on.parity(both.parities, end.of.both,
                            terminal.screen, odd.parity)
    end.of.odd.parity ! ANY

  consume(odd.parity, end.of.odd.parity)
```

In this particular case, the gain in modularity may not seem ade-
quate to justify the expense, both in programming effort and execution time. The advantage is clearer in cases where the program
must perform a number of tasks each of which divides its input data
into chunks, and where the boundaries of these components do not
coincide.

Using parallelism to resolve structure clash

A structure clash happens whenever a program must perform operations on data that must be divided into mutually overlapping components. In a text processing program, for example, it may prove
necessary to do something to every line of a document, and something else to every sentence.

The natural way to code each of these tasks, individually, is to
write programs whose structure reflects the structure of the document. To perform an action on every line:

```
WHILE ... there are more lines
  SEQ
    ... read a line
    ... process the line
```

and to perform an action on every sentence:

```
WHILE ... there are more sentences
  SEQ
    ... read a sentence
    ... process the sentence
```

Since sentences do not need to contain only complete lines, nor lines complete sentences, it is difficult to combine these two programs in a single sequential program. The somewhat unsatisfactory best that can be done in a sequential program is to treat the document as a sequence of words, these being the largest common sub-components of both lines and sentences.

```
WHILE ... there are more words
  SEQ
    ... read a word
    ... if it completes a line process the line
    ... if it completes a sentence process the sentence
```

In a parallel program, the structure of both component processes can be retained by performing the two divisions of the document concurrently

```
CHAN lines, sentences :
PAR
    ... copy the document to lines and sentences

  WHILE ... there are more lines
    SEQ
      ... read a line from lines
      ... process the line

  WHILE ... there are more sentences
    SEQ
      ... read a sentence from sentences
      ... process the sentence
```

The simplest case of a structure clash arises from attempting to pack data into fixed sized blocks that will not accommodate an exact whole number of items. It might be necessary, for example, to pack a stream of characters into half-kilobyte blocks for transmission or storage on a medium which accepts only such blocks. Consider first a case in which there is no structure clash: the medium is represented as a channel that accepts only slice outputs of half a kilobyte, and characters are represented by codes in the range from 0 to 255, so that a whole number of characters exactly fill a block.

The way to perform actions sequentially on the components of an array of bytes declared by

```
VAR buffer[BYTE bytes.in.a.block] :
```

is to use a sequential 'array' of processes created by the constructor

```
SEQ byte.number = [0 FOR bytes.in.a.block]
```

so this packing might be done by a process of the form

```
PROC pack.bytes.into.blocks(CHAN byte.source,
                            end.of.source, block.sink) =
   VAR more.bytes.expected :
   SEQ
     more.bytes.expected := TRUE
     WHILE more.bytes.expected
       VAR buffer[BYTE bytes.in.a.block] :
       SEQ
         SEQ byte.number = [0 FOR bytes.in.a.block]
           ALT
             more.bytes.expected &
                 byte.source ? buffer[BYTE byte.number]
               SKIP
             more.bytes.expected & end.of.source ? ANY
               more.bytes.expected := FALSE
             NOT more.bytes.expected & SKIP
               SKIP
         block.sink!buffer[BYTE 0 FOR bytes.in.a.block]:
```

The branch of the alternative that does all the work is the first, that guarded by an input from *byte.source* which inputs the next byte into the particular component of the buffer which is being considered. Since the guard does all the work, there is nothing left to be done in the guarded process, so this is SKIP. The condition before the SKIP guard ensures that it is ready when and only when there are no more bytes to be packed into the last block.

That process always sends a partly or completely empty block as its last output. The sending of a completely empty block could be prevented by looking ahead for the next byte:

```
DEF bytes.in.a.block = 512 :

PROC pack.bytes.into.blocks(CHAN byte.source,
                             end.of.source, block.sink) =
  -- Copy data from byte.source into complete blocks on
  -- block.sink, until there a signal arrives on
  -- end.of.source
  VAR next.byte :
  ALT
    byte.source ? next.byte     -- Read ahead first byte
      VAR more.bytes.to.pack :
      SEQ
        more.bytes.to.pack := TRUE
        WHILE more.bytes.to.pack
          DEF block.size  = bytes.in.a.block,
              buffer.size = block.size + 1   :
          VAR buffer[BYTE buffer.size] :
          SEQ
            buffer[BYTE 0] := next.byte
            SEQ byte.number = [1 FOR bytes.in.a.block]
              ALT
                more.bytes.to.pack &
                  byte.source?buffer[BYTE byte.number]
                  SKIP
                more.bytes.to.pack &
                  end.of.source ? ANY
                  more.bytes.to.pack := FALSE
                NOT more.bytes.to.pack & SKIP
                  SKIP
            block.sink ! buffer[BYTE 0 FOR block.size]
            next.byte := buffer[BYTE block.size]

    end.of.source ? ANY                -- No bytes at all
      SKIP                                               :
```

Even so, in case the entire message does not exactly fill a whole number of blocks, it has to be possible for a process that unpacks the characters from the blocks to deduce from those characters that it has reached the actual end of the character stream before the end of the last block.

Now consider the problem of trying to achieve a higher packing density, given that only character codes less than 128 are going to be sent, so that seven bits will suffice rather than eight. Seven bit values will not fit neatly into bytes, nor into half-kilobyte blocks. The problem can, however, be decomposed into two simpler separate problems in which there is no structure clash: turning seven bit character values into a sequence of bits, and packing a sequence of bits into blocks.

The packing of bits into blocks can be done in almost exactly the same way as that suggested for packing bytes into blocks. A byte can be considered to be an array of bits, indexed by using the bit-pattern manipulating operations. The assignment

```
buffer[BYTE byte.n] := buffer[BYTE byte.n] /\
                             (NOT (1 << bit.n))
```

sets the $bit.n^{\text{th}}$ bit of the $byte.n^{\text{th}}$ byte of *buffer* to zero, whilst

```
buffer[BYTE byte.n] := buffer[BYTE byte.n] \/
                             (1 << bit.n)
```

sets that same bit to one, so the conditional

```
PROC set.bit(VAR buffer[], VALUE byte.n, bit.n, bit) =
  IF
    bit = 0
      buffer[BYTE byte.n] := buffer[BYTE byte.n] /\
                                   (NOT (1 << bit.n))
    bit = 1
      buffer[BYTE byte.n] := buffer[BYTE byte.n] \/
                                   (1 << bit.n):
```

stores the given bit in the $bit.n^{\text{th}}$ bit of the $byte.n^{\text{th}}$ byte of the buffer. The buffer is being treated as a two-dimensional array, and the process that packs the buffer is a two-dimensional SEQ-FOR array of processes.

```
DEF bits.in.a.byte = 8, bytes.in.a.block = 512 :

PROC pack.bits.into.blocks(CHAN bit.source,
                           end.of.source, block.sink) =
  -- Copy data from bit.source in complete blocks onto
  -- block.sink, until there a signal arrives on
  -- end.of.source
  VAR next.bit :
  ALT
    bit.source ? next.bit    -- Read ahead the first bit
      VAR more.bits.to.pack :
      SEQ
        more.bits.to.pack := TRUE
        WHILE more.bits.to.pack
          DEF block.size = bytes.in.a.block :
          VAR buffer[BYTE block.size] :
          SEQ
            SEQ byte.number = [0 FOR bits.in.a.block]
              IF
                more.bits.to.pack
                  SEQ bit.number=[0 FOR bits.in.a.byte]
                    IF
                      more.bits.to.pack
                        SEQ
                          set.bit(buffer, byte.number,
                                  bit.number, next.bit)
                          ALT
                            bit.source ? next.bit
                              SKIP
                            end.of.source ? ANY
                              more.bits.to.pack:= FALSE
                      NOT more.bits.to.pack
                        SKIP
                NOT more.bits.to.pack
                  SKIP
            block.sink ! buffer[BYTE 0 FOR block.size]
    end.of.source ? ANY              -- No bits at all
      SKIP                                              :
```

Turning seven bit characters into a sequence of bits is also a simple task, since there is again no structure clash. The value of the expression

```
(character >> bit.number) /\ 1
```

is zero or one according to the value of the *bit.number*[th] bit of the
value of character, so the character code can be treated as though it
were an array of seven bits.

```
DEF bits.in.a.character = 7 :

SEQ bit.number = [0 FOR bits.in.a.character]
  bit.sink ! (character >> bit.number) /\ 1
```

The process to turn a stream of characters into a stream of the
bits which make up their codes, least significant bit of the character
first, has the same structure as the earlier unpacking processes:

```
DEF bits.in.a.character = 7 :

PROC unpack.bits.from.characters(CHAN char.source,
                                 end.of.source, bit.sink) =
  -- Copy characters from char.source a bit at a time
  -- onto bit.sink, until a signal arrives on
  -- end.of.source
  VAR more.characters.expected :
  SEQ
    more.characters.expected := TRUE
    WHILE more.characters.expected
      VAR character :
      ALT
        char.source ? character
          SEQ bit.number = [0 FOR bits.in.a.character]
            bit.sink ! (character >> bit.number) /\ 1
        end.of.source ? ANY
          more.characters.expected := FALSE          :
```

Packing seven bit characters into half-kilobyte blocks is simply a
matter of unpacking the characters into a stream of bits, and assem-
bling the blocks from the stream of bits, the one activity in parallel
with the other.

```
DEF bits.in.a.character =   7,
    bits.in.a.byte      =   8,
    bytes.in.a.block    = 512 :

PROC pack.characters.into.blocks(CHAN char.source,
                          end.of.source, block.sink) =

  PROC unpack.bits.from.characters(CHAN char.source,
                            end.of.source, bit.sink) =
    ... Send of character codes from char.source
    ... a bit at a time along bit.sink

  PROC pack.bits.into.blocks(CHAN bit.source,
                          end.of.source, block.sink) =
    ... Pack bits from bit.source into complete
    ... blocks and send them along block.sink

  CHAN bit.stream, end.of.bit.stream :
  PAR
    SEQ
      unpack.bits.from.characters(char.source,
                      end.of.source, bit.stream)
      end.of.bit.stream ! ANY

    pack.bits.into.blocks(bit.stream,
                  end.of.bit.stream, block.sink) :
```

Substantially the same program structure can clearly be used to turn the stream of blocks back into a stream of seven bit character codes, since that is just another, similar packing problem. The solution to each packing problem is of one of the three forms that I have shown here: grouping small objects to make larger ones; dividing large objects to make small ones; or a problem in which a structure clash requires that both the input data and the output data be divided into common sub-components.

3 Local time

There are many applications of programmed devices where it is necessary for the program to be able to refer to, or to measure, the passage of time: for example, in long-distance communication, the participants are usually prepared to wait for replies for a limited time only, before taking action to recover from the loss of messages. To accommodate these needs, there are two primitive processes by which *occam* programs may refer to the changing state of a local clock. I mention them here to complete the presentation, but they will hardly be used in the programs which follow: you may want to pass by this section on a first reading.

The clock reading process

```
TIME ? variable
```

sets the value of the variable to the current reading on the clock. This is a word-sized bit pattern which changes at a uniform rate with the passage of time, the rate of change being dependent on the particular implementation. It counts up cyclically through a set of values distributed through the whole range of bit patterns, the most negative reading following after the most positive one. Notice that it is misleading for this process to look like an input process: the sequence of symbols ⎡TIME ?⎤ is semantically indivisible, TIME is not a channel, nor are clock reading processes governed by the rules that control the legal uses of channels: many concurrent processes may legally read the time from the same clock.

The clock delay process

```
TIME ? AFTER expression
```

is another process that does nothing, like `SKIP`, except that it may suspend execution. It does not terminate until the reading on the clock has satisfied the condition

```
reading AFTER expression
```

I have been careful in the wording of that last sentence: notice that there is no guarantee about the value of *variable* after the execution of

```
SEQ
  TIME ? AFTER expression
  TIME ? variable
```

As before, the sequence of symbols TIME ? AFTER is atomic, a delay is not an input process, but it is allowed to stand in the place of an input process as a guard of an alternative. Such a guard becomes ready as soon as the delay process may terminate.

The operator `AFTER` is intended for the comparison of readings taken from the clock. Provided that two times are separated by less than half the time that it takes for the clock to count around the complete cycle of its readings, one time is after the other if readings taken from the clock at those times are similarly related by `AFTER`. The cycle time of the clock depends on the word size, on the amount by which the reading is incremented at each tick, and the frequency of the clock ticks. Each of these depends on the particular implementation, and I will assume that you can supply a definition

```
DEF second = ...
```

in any program that needs it, indicating by how much the reading changes in one second. (This assumption will be unjustified if the clock cycle time is two seconds or less, as might be the case on a device with short words and a fast ticking clock.)

Any two readings being compared, either directly, or by the delay process, should be taken from the same clock: the language does not guarantee any relationship between readings taken in different branches of a `PAR` construct. Notionally, the clock is a register on a transputer, and no connection is to be expected between that register and the registers of any other transputers participating in the execution of a program. There is no mechanism in the language which maintains a global time, and it is the programmer's responsibility to implement one if it is needed. Similarly, if needed it is the programmer's task to provide a mechanism, using the clock, for timing long periods (those in excess of half a clock cycle time).

There are three idioms that, in combination, encompass almost all uses of the clock. First of all, to suspend execution for a fixed time, say ten seconds

```
VAR started :
SEQ
  TIME ? started
  TIME ? AFTER started + (10 * second)
```

This might happen as a once-only action in a program while starting or stopping some mechanical peripheral device.

If an action is to be performed at regular intervals, say once every ten seconds, then

```
VAR next.dead.line :
SEQ
  TIME ? next.dead.line
  WHILE ...
    SEQ
      next.dead.line := next.dead.line + (10 * second)
      TIME ? AFTER next.dead.line
      ... perform action
```

will do this (provided that the action can be completed in under ten seconds!) Notice that each deadline is set relative to the previous deadline, so as to avoid slippage.

Finally, using delay guards allows a process to limit the time for which it is prepared to wait for input.

```
VAR prompted, ch :
SEQ
  write.string(terminal.screen, "Yer wot? ")
  TIME ? prompted
  ALT
    terminal.keyboard ? ch
      to.program ! ch
    TIME ? AFTER prompted + (30 * second)
      to.program ! operator.asleep.or.dead
```

Provided that the input from the *terminal.keyboard* arrives within thirty seconds of the clock being read, the alternative will select its

first guard. After that time, the other guard is ready and the process
is no longer obliged to wait for its input.

4 Formatted input and output

One of the things that you will probably miss in *occam* if you are used to programming in a typed high level language is the support for text input and output. There are usually either predefined routines, or language constructs, which take your program's data, such as strings, integers, floating point numbers, and translate them into sequences of characters for output to terminals and printers. Similarly, there are usually routines provided for reading sequences of digits, and interpreting them as numbers, and so on. It is almost always possible for you to write your own input and output routines, but those provided for you will usually do.

Since *occam* programs are, at least notionally, to run as 'stand alone' programs, there is no standard operating system or run-time library of such support routines, and the input and output translations must be performed by the program. Moreover, since there is no type information in the program, no standard routine can 'know' that you are interpreting a particular bit-pattern as a character code, or as a signed integer, or perhaps as a floating point number. Each program needs specific processes which translate those types of value whose text representations are input and output by that program.

This section introduces sequential input and output routines used in programs later in the book, and some others which you may find useful.

Output routines

A process for outputting the characters of a string appeared earlier, in the 'Programming structures'

```
PROC write.string(CHAN output, VALUE string[]) =
  -- Write the characters of the string[] to the output
  SEQ character.number = [1 FOR string[BYTE 0]]
    output ! string[BYTE character.number]          :
```

You will also probably need to output bit patterns as decimal numerals. If you have ever written this routine before, there ought to be no difficulty, except that an *occam* process cannot use recursion.

First of all, if *tens* is a power of ten then '0' + ((n/tens)\10) is the digit of that weight in the numeral representing the positive integer *n*. Notice that '0' is just the character code for zero: in the addition it is treated as any other bit-pattern. The result becomes a character again only in as much as that you will choose to treat it as one by, for example, outputting it to a terminal.

To output the whole numeral for *n* the digit calculation must be performed for each power of ten not exceeding *n*, and the results are required in sequence in decreasing order of their weight.

```
VAR tens :
SEQ
  tens := 1
  WHILE (n / tens) >= 10
    tens := 10 * tens
  WHILE tens > 0
    SEQ
      output ! '0' + ((n / tens) \ 10)
      tens := tens / 10
```

The division of *tens* by ten always gives an exact answer, excepting the final occasion, when *tens* is one, and the result of the divison is zero. That process works for all positive *n* and, as a special case, for zero.

It is tempting to try outputting negative numbers by first changing the sign, but this is wrong, because changing the sign of the most negative number gives no defined result. Whatever the effect, it cannot possibly give the right answer, since that is not a representable value. The standard, if perhaps confusing, solution is to treat positive numbers as special cases which are best output by making them negative, or equivalently, to change the sign of *tens*, so that the result of dividing by *tens* is consistently negative.

```
PROC write.signed(CHAN output, VALUE n) =
  -- Write a signed decimal representation of n
  -- to the output channel
  VAR tens :
  SEQ
    IF
      n < 0
        SEQ
          output ! '-'
          tens := 1
      n >= 0
        tens := -1
    WHILE (n / tens) <= (-10)
      tens := 10 * tens
    WHILE tens <> 0
      SEQ
        output ! '0' - ((n / tens) \ 10)
        tens := tens / 10                      :
```

Notice that it is a matter of the definition of the division and remainder operators in *occam* that changing the sign either of *tens* or of *n* just changes the sign of the expression $((n/tens)\backslash 10)$.

None of the expressions in the process have results outside the range of representable integers: for example, the result of the multiplication 10 * tens in the first loop is guaranteed, by the condition on the loop, to be no further from zero than is *n*, so the multiplication gives the correct result. Similarly, the condition on that loop has to be written in that way, because calculating, say $(-(n/tens))>=10$ might involve negating the most negative number.

As a final sophistication to this process, you might want to send leading spaces so that the numeral occupies a fixed number of character spaces, to simplify the laying out of columns of numbers. The simplest way of doing this is to count the digits whilst calculating the value of *tens*.

```
PROC write.signed(CHAN output, VALUE n, field.width) =
  ... Write a signed decimal representation of n
  ... to the output, right justified to occupy
  ... field.width character spaces
```

A coding of this process appears at the beginning of the collection of codes of the programs.

Input routines

Constructing a data object from its textual representation is slightly more difficult because, in general, not all sequences of characters will be legal representations. For example, a process to read a numeral might expect some spaces, perhaps a sign and some more spaces, and then a sequence of digits, followed by something else. If there are no digits, or if the number represented is too large to be encoded as a bit-pattern, then an error has occurred.

The particular action to be taken to recover from an error depends on the circumstances of the conversion: for example, whether the digits are being read from a terminal keyboard, or a magnetic tape, whether the process is running in a desk-top microcomputer or in aircraft auto-pilot equipment. For a general purpose routine, I will settle for returning a Boolean indication of whether the conversion was successful. (Other indications might be possible, for example, a communication on a channel laid aside for indicating errors.)

Ignoring, for the present, the matter of the sign, and the possibility of error, a sequence of digits can be converted into a bit-pattern representing the same number by

```
VAR ch :
SEQ
  n := 0
  input ? ch
  WHILE ('0' <= ch) AND (ch <= '9')
    SEQ
      n := (10 * n) + (ch - '0')
      input ? ch
```

The arithmetic is essentially dual to that in the output routine. If *ch* is the character code of a digit, then it lies between the codes of the characters zero and nine, and (ch − '0') is its value as a digit.

As in the case of output, it is necessary to be careful with the most negative integer: it will not do to read negative numerals by reading the digits as if they were those of a positive numeral and then changing the sign of the result. The simplest solution to this problem is to change the sign of each digit before accumulation, keeping *n* negative throughout.

So as to check for overflow, the new value of *n* must be compared with either the most positive or the most negative bit-pattern, again being careful to keep all the arithmetic in the expressible range.

```
DEF min = NOT ((NOT 0) >> 1), max = (NOT 0) >> 1 :

IF
  (sign = '+') AND (n <= ((max - (ch - '0')) / 10))
    n := (10 * n) + (ch - '0')
  (sign = '-') AND (((min + (ch - '0')) / 10) <= n)
    n := (10 * n) - (ch - '0')
  otherwise
    ok := FALSE     -- an error has occurred
```

A possible solution to the problem of errors would be to omit the third branch of the conditional entirely, so that the routine would become deadlocked in case of an overflow. This more general solution postpones the decision, giving the caller of the process the option of ignoring the error, or of acting on it in any way he chooses, including the option of stopping.

The appendix contains a routine complementary to *write.signed* which has the following specification:

```
PROC read.signed(CHAN input, VAR n, ok) =
  ... Read an (optionally signed) decimal numeral from
  ... the input returning the corresponding value in n,
  ... and TRUE or FALSE in ok according as the
  ... conversion worked or not
```

In many programming languages a routine like *read.signed* could only be used for conversion of a numeral being read from a peripheral device. In PASCAL, for example, such a routine would be reading from a file, but an entirely different routine would be needed to convert a numeral stored in an array of characters. In *occam*, there is nothing to stop you doing this by putting input and output routines together in parallel. The process

```
CHAN internal :
PAR
  write.string(internal, "-137*C")
  read.signed(internal, n, ok)
```

sets n to -137. This might not look very useful for constant strings, but the same can be done with variable arrays of characters. This means, for example, that it is easy to separate the business of line construction, editing and echoing when reading from a terminal, from whatever data conversion you might want to perform on the input.

For completeness, the appendix also contains a coding of a line construction process suitable for input from a VDU

```
PROC read.line(CHAN keyboard, screen, VAR s[]) =
   ... Construct a string in s[] from the printable
   ... characters read from keyboard and echoed to
   ... screen. The string finishes at a carriage return.
```

As it reads characters from the *keyboard* stream, this process packs them into the byte array *s*[ ] and echoes them to the *screen* stream, allowing the usual sort of line editing. For example, typing backspace

```
SEQ
   keyboard ? ch
   IF
      :
      (ch = backspace) AND (s[BYTE 0] > 0)
         SEQ
            screen ! backspace ; '*s' ; backspace
            s[BYTE 0] := s[BYTE 0] - 1
      :
```

cancels the last character in the line, and removes its echo from the screen by writing a blank in its place.

5   In place of interrupts

It used to be that programmers only met concurrently executing processes if they had to code interrupt routines, or to write code which shared store with interrupt routines. An interrupt is a mechanism designed to make small amounts of processing power available at short notice to handle urgent tasks, when it would be unreasonably expensive to make that processing capability permanently available. To this extent, it separates two concerns: an applications programmer wanting to send characters to a lineprinter need only supply them to an interrupt handler; it is the responsibility of the interrupt handler to transmit them to the printer at the precise times that the printer indicates that it is ready for them. In this way, the programmer is relieved of the burden of making frequent checks on the state of the printer, and the structure of his program can be unaffected by the timing constraints imposed by the printer.

Interrupt routines are notoriously difficult to code and to use. In addition to assuming responsibilities of meeting real-time deadlines, the interrupt routine must maintain the programmer's illusion that the application program has exclusive use of the processor and store. This imposes rigorous discipline on the use of registers, and of store locations, both to avoid conflicts, and in the management of those shared variables by which program and interrupt routine communicate. Moreover, the interrupt routine has usually to be programmed as a 'subroutine' (rather than a 'coroutine') invoked once by each interrupt, which means that any state that is to persist from the handling of one interrupt to that of the next must be saved in store and reconstructed at the next interrupt. To make matters worse, high level programming languages are rarely able to offer convenient abstractions for coding interrupt handlers, which are inherently machine-dependent, and it is usual for interrupt routines to be written in machine code.

It is tempting to claim that the concurrently executed processes of *occam* are the right tools for writing interrupt routines. To do so would be misleading: concurrent processes are right for a task for which interrupt routines have always been inadequate! The task is in two parts: that of writing code to meet real-time deadlines; and that of isolating their effects, so as to keep the rest of the program simple.

In *occam*, sustaining the illusion that the application program has exclusive use of the processor and store is easily done, since each and every process of every *occam* program operates under this very illusion. The illusion is sufficiently strong that a programmer need never know whether or not any particular process is executed on its own dedicated processor.

Meeting real-time deadlines remains a problem that must be solved by ensuring that each processor is fast enough, and that the code is short enough. Apart from this concern with urgency, an interrupt handler coded in *occam* can be written in exactly the same way as any other process, and communicates with the application program in the same way as any other processes communicate with each other.

Managing terminal input

To take a concrete example, consider managing the traffic to and from a terminal. Every time a key is struck at the keyboard, there will be a corresponding event (traditionally an interrupt) in the computer, and some action must be taken to read information about the key before the next key is struck, lest the information be lost. Quite often the action taken will be to store the character corresponding to the key in a buffer, from which it will subsequently be read at the leisure of the program which is consuming the terminal input. The capacity of the buffer determines how many characters can be 'typed ahead' of the demand from the program.

In *occam*, an 'event in the computer' is represented by a communication on a special channel. Special channels are declared by noting some implementation-dependent value (such as the store address of the relevant peripheral controller) in the declaration,

```
CHAN keystroke.in AT 32540 :
```

Programs use special channels just as they would use other channels, except that they use each channel only for input, or only for output, with the other half of the communication being performed by a process implemented in the hardware. On a transputer, this would be a 'link' to some other device.

In the case of the terminal example it would be possible, every time a key was struck, for the program to perform an input

```
keystroke.in ? ch
```

so a reasonable interrupt handler might be

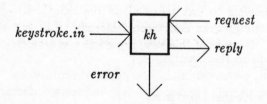

```
circular.buffer(keystroke.in, request, reply)
```

using the circular buffer coded in the 'Programming structures' section. This process has the disadvantage that, were the buffer to become full through the coincidence of a fast typist and a slow program, the process would no longer be prepared to accept input from *keystroke.in*. Since there is (fortunately) no mechanism built into present-day terminals to suspend the execution of the typist while the computer is busy, this would mean that keystrokes made whilst the buffer was full would be lost, without warning.

An improved scheme would be to code the interrupt handler in such a way that it was always prepared to acknowledge the keystroke, and to take some remedial action in case there were no room left in the buffer.

This process will signal on the *error* channel if an attempt is made to overfill the type-ahead buffer; later, I will use that signal to cause the bell on the terminal to be rung.

```
PROC keyboard.handler(CHAN request, sink, error) =
  -- Characters typed at the keyboard can be read from
  -- sink. A signal is required on request before each
  -- item is read. If more than type.ahead are typed
  -- ahead, an error is signalled.
  CHAN keystroke.in AT ... :
  VAR reader, writer, count :
  SEQ
    reader := 0
    writer := 0
    count  := type.ahead
    VAR datum[type.ahead] :
    WHILE TRUE
      ALT
        count = 0     &    keystroke.in ? ANY
          error ! ANY
        count > 0     &    keystroke.in ? datum[writer]
          SEQ
            writer  := (writer + 1) \ type.ahead
            count   := count - 1
        count < type.ahead   &    request ? ANY
          SEQ
            sink ! datum[reader]
            reader  := (reader + 1) \ type.ahead
            count   := count + 1                      :
```

Notice that the *keyboard.handler* is written in such a way that, provided

◊ the outputs to error and sink are never delayed for more than a fixed time

◊ this process executes at a known rate within a known short time of becoming ready

then it is possible to put a bound on the length of time which can pass before the process next becomes ready to accept an input from *keystroke.in.* Bounds of this kind are what you would need to demonstrate that no interrupts were lost.

Managing terminal output

For the purpose of this example, suppose that the outgoing traffic to the terminal screen consists of a sequence of bytes passing along the special channel *screen.out* to be displayed as characters on a screen,

or acted upon in some other way by the terminal. The terminal may
then become busy for some short time, before again being ready to
accept output. The screen handling process has to accept characters
from the user's program, and to pass them on; additionally, it must
accept urgent error signals from the process handling the type-ahead
buffer, and send a 'bell' character to the terminal when an error is
flagged.

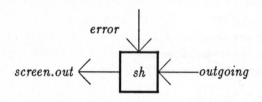

```
DEF control = NOT ((NOT 0) << 5) :

PROC screen.handler(CHAN outgoing, error) =
  DEF bell.character = control /\ 'G' :
  CHAN screen.out AT ... :
  WHILE TRUE
    VAR ch :
    ALT
      outgoing ? ch
        screen.out ! ch
      error ? ANY
        screen.out ! bell.character                :
```

It might appear that there are no timing constraints on the behaviour of the screen handling process, but recall that the perfor-
mance of the *keyboard.handler* depends on its *error* signals not being
unduly delayed. As written, the *error*-guard in the *screen.handler*
might indeed be delayed indefinitely, even were it guaranteed that
the *screen.handler* was executed immediately either of the guards became ready. It might be that the process that sends characters along
the *outgoing* channel is able to send a new character in less time than
it takes the *screen.handler* to execute the body of its WHILE loop once.
In that case, the *outgoing*-guard would always be ready every time
the alternative was executed, and since an alternative can choose any
one of the ready guards, it is possible that the *error*-guard might
be ignored indefinitely, even were it ready. Notice, particularly, that
this behaviour is not caused by my having written the *outgoing*-guard

first: the order of the components of an alternative is immaterial to its meaning.

For just this reason some implementations of *occam* have an additional constructor, PRI ALT, which breaks the symmetry. (PRI is meant to be read *prioritized*!) The components of an asymmetric alternative are of the same sort as those of the symmetric construct, but the meaning differs in that earlier components are treated more favourably than later ones. The alternative waits until one of its guards is ready, then the earliest (nearest to the top of the paper) of the ready guards is selected. Execution of the selected component is then the same as it would be in a symmetric alternative. This means that if the *screen.handler* were re-written

```
PROC screen.handler(CHAN outgoing, error) =
  DEF bell.character = control /\ 'G' :
  CHAN screen.out AT ... :
  WHILE TRUE
    VAR ch :
    PRI ALT
      error ? ANY
        screen.out ! bell.character
      outgoing ? ch
        screen.out ! ch                    :
```

then an *error* signal could not be delayed for longer than it takes to execute the body of the WHILE loop once. Discharging the responsibility to accept these signals in a fixed time reduces to showing that

⋄ the outputs to *screen.out* are never delayed for more than a fixed time

⋄ this process executes at a known rate within a known short time of becoming ready

The first requirement is met by the terminal, by assumption; to the second I will return later. Notice that there is no constraint on the timing of transactions on the *outgoing* channel; I am building a firewall around the terminal, beyond which meeting real-time deadlines will no longer be a concern.

A particular program that uses the terminal may contain a large number of processes, each needing to send characters to the terminal screen. Since the *outgoing* channel is now the only way out to the terminal, and since only one process is able to send along that channel, a process must be written to interleave the many output streams, and send their interleaving along *outgoing*.

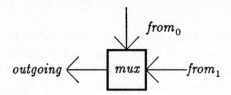

```
DEF release = -1 :

PROC output.multiplexer(CHAN from[], VALUE width,
                                        CHAN outgoing) =
  WHILE TRUE
    VAR ch :
    ALT selected.process = [0 FOR width]
      from[selected.process] ? ch
        WHILE ch <> release
          SEQ
            outgoing ! ch
            from[selected.process] ? ch           :
```

This process interleaves messages (sequences of characters) from each
of the *from*[ ] channels, in an arbitrary order, each message being
terminated by the *release* value. The most interesting property of
this process, for our present purpose, is that it is outside the firewall:
there are no constraints on the speed with which it executes, nor on
the times at which other processes communicate with it.

Managing echoing

The time-dependency firewall is not yet complete: there remains the
problem of reading from the type-ahead buffer. Recall that, having
issued a *request* signal, the reader assumes a responsibility to accept
the reply from the *sink* channel within a fixed time. That means the
reader must be within the firewall.

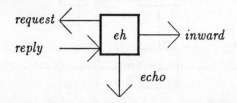

This process reads characters from the type-ahead buffer by signalling
a *request* and accepting a *reply*. The character is passed on to the

inward channel to the user. I have given this process the additional job of 'echoing' the printable characters to the terminal screen as and when they are read by the program using the keyboard input.

```
PROC echo.handler(CHAN request, reply, echo, inward) =
  DEF enter = control /\ 'M' :
  WHILE TRUE
    VAR ch :
    SEQ
      request ! ANY
      reply ? ch
      inward ! ch     -- Transmit character to user
      IF
        ('*s' <= ch)  AND  (ch <= '~')
                        -- Echo visible input to screen
          echo ! ch
        ch = enter      -- Release screen at end of line
          echo ! release
        TRUE            -- No action on other characters
          SKIP                                            :
```

The only timing constraint on this process is that it execute sufficiently rapidly that the input from *reply* is accepted within a permissible time of acceptance by the *keyboard.handler* of the preceding *request*. There being no constraints on communication on the *echo* and *inward* channels, these may cross the firewall: the *echo* channel is to be one of the array *from*[ ] going to the *screen.multiplexer*, and the *inward* channel can be used directly by the process that consumes keyboard input.

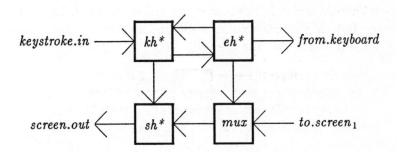

The starred processes are ones that have to execute at a known rate within a known time of being ready. Notice that the screen sharing

strategy is implemented by an 'ordinary' process not subject to any timing constraints. Since each line of echoed characters from the type-ahead buffer is sent to the screen as an indivisible message, there is no problem about input characters being mixed in with output, but neither is there any need for the *echo.handler* to be concerned with screen allocation.

If the program that used the terminal were written as the named process *user*, then the whole could be put together with the terminal handler

```
DEF type.ahead = ...,
    control    = NOT ((NOT 0) << 5),
    release    = -1 :

PROC keyboard.handler(CHAN request, sink, error) =
    ...
PROC echo.handler(CHAN request, reply, echo, inward) =
    ...
PROC output.multiplexer(CHAN from[], VALUE width,
                                        CHAN outgoing) =
    ...
PROC screen.handler(CHAN outgoing, error) =
    ...
PROC user(CHAN terminal.keyboard, terminal.screen) =
    ...


CHAN request, reply, error, outgoing, from.keyboard :
DEF from.echo.handler = 0,
    from.user          = 1,
    number.of.outputs = 2 :
CHAN to.screen[number.of.outputs] :

PAR
    keyboard.handler(request, reply, error)               --*
    echo.handler(request, reply,
        to.screen[from.echo.handler], from.keyboard)      --*
    output.multiplexer(to.screen, number.of.outputs,
                                        outgoing)
    screen.handler(outgoing, error)                       --*
    user(from.keyboard, to.screen[from.user])
```

Configuration directives

Ignoring, for the moment, the timing constraints imposed by the proper handling of the terminal interrupts, checking the correctness of this program can be done in two parts. First of all, there are properties of individual processes that can be checked in isolation from the other processes: for example, that the *echo.handler* performs a cycle of four communications in a fixed order, behaviour that is unaffected by the other processes. Secondly, there are some properties that are inherently global, notably freedom from deadlock, which may depend on the behaviour of every one of the processes.

The same is the case with the timing constraints: the argument thus far has been about each of the component processes, more or less in isolation. Had I settled on a particular implementation of *occam* on a particular computer, and on a particular set of terminal characteristics, then I could have calculated the 'fixed times' within which actions must occur as so many seconds of processor time, so much communication time, and so on. It remains, however, to be demonstrated that there will always be sufficient processor time available when it is required.

One way of achieving this would be to dedicate a processor to the execution of each of the five components of the program. Dialects of *occam* intended for writing such multi-processor programs have a variant of the parallel constructor, PLACED PAR, for indicating such a division of labour. Were this used in place of the PAR in the present program, then the processor occupancy times calculated for the three starred processes would be actual elapsed times, each independent of the processor loading of the other processes. In this particular case, such a solution seems excessive, since the tasks are each fairly simple, and the traffic is light. It would be a more reasonable way of dealing with, say, the traffic to and from a fast disk, where a whole transputer might be allocated to managing the large volumes of data, and the potentially intricate calculations required to make efficient accesses to the disk.

More realistically, this particular program would probably be run on a single processor, say one transputer. As it stands, in order to be able to guarantee sufficient speed of execution in the starred processes, I must know details of the behaviour of the unstarred processes: for example, that the *user* process does not require more than a known propertion of the processor's time. This being unsatisfactory, there is another dialectal variant of PAR, one which distinguishes more and less urgent tasks. As with asymmetric alternative the asymmetric parallel construct, constructed with PRI PAR, is made of the same components as the symmetric variant, but differs in execution by favouring its earlier components. For example, the process

```
PRI PAR
  p
  q
  r
```

executes by the concurrent execution of its three components, but *q* can only execute when *p* is prevented from doing so because it is waiting for a communication or has already terminated. Similarly, *r* can only execute when both *p* and *q* are blocked, and execution of *r* will rapidly be suspended should either of the higher priority processes become ready.

The asymmetric parallel constructor, if used, must be the outermost constructor of a uni-processor program, or the outermost constructor of one of the branches of a PLACED parallel construct. In *occam* programs to be executed on currently proposed transputers, asymmetric parallel constructs can have no more than two components, corresponding to the two process-queues in the transputer. For that machine, the right way to organize the terminal handler would be

```
PRI PAR
  PAR                                    -- High priority process
    keyboard.handler(request, reply, error)
    echo.handler(request, reply,
            to.screen[from.echo.handler], from.keyboard)
    screen.handler(outgoing, error)
  PAR                                    -- Low priority process
    output.multiplexer(to.screen, number.of.outputs,
                                            outgoing)
    user(from.keyboard, to.screen[from.user])
```

Now it cannot matter what the *user* or *output.multiplexer* processes do: if any of the urgent processes is able to execute, then one of them will do so within a very short time. This latency will be determined and guaranteed by the implementation, so again if I had a particular implementation in mind, this would be known. The total waiting time, for any of the 'interrupt' processes, between becoming ready and beginning to execute, is bounded by the sum of one latency time and the sum of the longest execution time of each of the other interrupt processes.

That completes the analysis of the timing of the program. All that is needed in the case of a particular implementation is to calculate the times, a matter of counting instructions, which task could and should be delegated to the compiler. Substituting the figures for the waiting and execution times allows a check to be made that the required response times are achieved.

6   Parallel matrix multiplication

In systems which manipulate and display geometrical data, one of the
common routine tasks is the application of linear transformations to
the data. A system containing a representation of a three-dimensional
object may need to rotate or displace that representation so as to
select a point of view from which to project a two-dimensional picture
of the object onto the plane of a terminal screen, or a plotter. If the
positions of the parts of the object are represented by a sequence of
Cartesian co-ordinates, then these rotations and displacements can be
achieved by matrix multiplication. For each point, with co-ordinates
$\langle x_0, x_1, x_2 \rangle$, it is necessary to calculate the corresponding transformed
co-ordinates $\langle y_0, y_1, y_2 \rangle$ given by

$$ y_i = \sum_{j=0}^{2} a_{ij} x_j + k_i $$

This requires nine multiplications and nine additions for each point
in the representation of the object.

If the transformation is being applied once to an object with a
view to printing an image on a slow, hard copy device such as a pen
plotter, then the time taken to do the transformation is probably not
important, and it does not matter much how the matrix multiplication is organized. On the other hand, if the image is being displayed
on a cathode ray tube, and the observer is allowed to change his point
of view from the console, then speed is important. Ideally, the transformation should be applied to every relevant point of the object as
the position of that point is required for refreshing the display, so

58

that the observer sees the effect of a change in the transformation as soon as possible.

If there are of the order of a thousand points in the representation of the image, then this means something of the order of a hundred thousand matrix multiplications in a second. For practical purposes, this requires that special hardware be dedicated to performing the matrix multiplications on a stream of co-ordinates on its way to the display. In such an arrangement, the time taken to perform the nine individual multiplications will dominate the time taken by all of the communications and additions involved. There is therefore an advantage in arranging that as many as possible of the multiplications can happen at once.

A natural configuration of processors to perform this task is a square array, mimicking the matrix a, one processor being responsible for each element of the matrix, and performing the multiplication by that element.

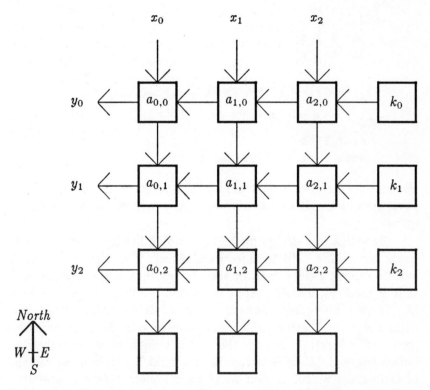

Successive values of each x co-ordinate are poured into the array from the top, passing down along the north to south channels, and successive values of the transformed *y* co-ordinates emerge from the east to west channels at the left of the array. In this diagram, each processor is labelled with the parameter for which it takes responsibility. For simplicity, the transformation is assumed to be constant: a mechanism for changing the parameter values might involve a further array of channels at right angles to the plane of the array of processes. These would connect each relevant processor to a controlling process.

Each multiplier cell has three tasks to perform during each complete matrix multiplication: getting the next co-ordinate x_j from its northern neighbour and passing it on to its southern neighbour; performing its own multiplication; getting a partial sum from its eastern neighbour, adding its own contribution and passing the sum on to the west. These tasks might be performed sequentially

```
VAR xj, aij.times.xj, yi :
WHILE TRUE
  SEQ
    SEQ
      north ? xj
      south ! xj

    aij.times.xj := aij * xj

    SEQ
      east ? yi
      west ! yi + aij.times.xj
```

Because the condition on the loop is a constant TRUE, this process never terminates; it repeatedly performs the three tasks in strict sequence.

Since this is a design for highly parallel hardware, it should be worth extracting a little more parallelism. The input from *north* has to happen before each of the actions that use the value of *xj* that is received, and the input from *east* has to precede the use of *yi*. There is no reason, however, to wait for the value of *yi* before doing the multiplication (which was assumed to be the most expensive part of the task). Similarly, the multiplication must be completed before the variable *xj* is reused for the next input from *north*, and of course the multiplication must be complete before its result is used in the addition. The process can be rearranged to 'overlap' the multiplication with activity of which it is independent, provided only that these constraints are respected.

```
PROC multiplier(VALUE aij,
                CHAN north, south, west, east) =
  VAR xj, aij.times.xj, yi :
  SEQ
    north ? xj
    WHILE TRUE
      SEQ
        PAR
          south ! xj
          aij.times.xj := aij * xj
          east ? yi
        PAR
          west ! yi + aij.times.xj
          north ? xj                              :
```

Since different components of a *multiplier* implemented in hardware would be used by the arithmetic and each of the communications, the branches of the PAR constructs naturally execute simultaneously.

Notice that the multiplier process does not need to know where it is in the array—it is independent of i and of j. This means that an implementation in hardware could use nine identical circuits.

In order to complete the matrix multiplier, a source of the k_i offset values is needed along the eastern border

```
PROC offset(VALUE ki, CHAN west) =
  WHILE TRUE
    west ! ki                              :
```

and a sink must be provided at the southern end of each column of multipliers to receive the redundant x_j from the southernmost multiplier processes

```
PROC sink(CHAN north) =
  WHILE TRUE
    north ? ANY              :
```

Although the *sink* does nothing with the values received, its input actions are necessary so that the corresponding output can happen in its neighbouring *multiplier*. A row of *sink* processes yields a simpler solution than one which involves two kinds of multiplier process, one for the north of the array, and another for the southernmost row.

Connecting these components to form the matrix multiplier is a matter of choosing an enumeration for the channels, and using CHAN arrays, suitably indexed. One solution is

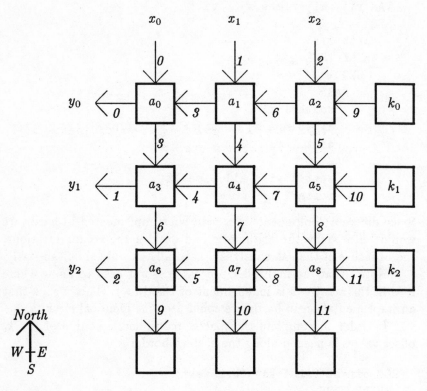

The channels connected to a typical multiplier process are

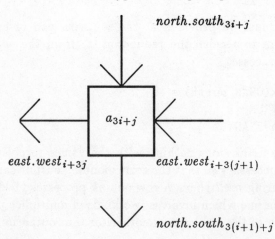

Elements of the matrix *a* have also been enumerated, so as to correspond to the elements of an *occam* one-dimensional array. The whole multiplier is described by the program

```
DEF n = 3 :
VAR a[n * n], k[n] :
SEQ
  -- initialize a and k

  CHAN north.south[(n+1)*n], east.west[n*(n+1)] :
  PAR
    PAR j = [0 FOR n]   -- producer of co-ordinates x[j]
      produce.xj(j, north.south[j])

    PAR                    -- the matrix multiplier
      PAR i = [0 FOR n]
        offset(k[i], east.west[(n*n)+i])
      PAR i = [0 FOR n]
        PAR j = [0 FOR n]
          multiplier( a[(n*i)+j],
                      north.south[(n * i) + j],
                      north.south[(n * (i + 1)) + j],
                      east.west  [i + (n * j)],
                      east.west  [i + (n * (j + 1))])
      PAR j = [0 FOR n]
        sink(north.south[(n*n)+j])

    PAR i = [0 FOR n]   -- consumer of co-ordinates y[i]
      consume.yi(i, east.west[i])
```

It is the task of each *produce.xj* process to output successive values of the co-ordinate corresponding to its first parameter, and that of each *consume.yi* process to input successive values of the transformed co-ordinate.

By devising suitable definitions for the processes *produce.xj* and *consume.yi*, this program can be used on any *occam* implementation as a simulation of the parallel matrix multiplier hardware. Of course, if it is executed on a single processor computer, then it will be very much slower than a simpler sequential program, because of the additional work in communicating and scheduling. On the special hardware for which it is designed, however, it would be very much faster. The longest data path from input to output is that traversed by x_2 on the way to contributing to y_2. This path involves six communications, three additions, and a single multiplication, all of which must happen in sequence. The program is designed on the assumption that the time taken for the multiplication would dominate all others, under which assumption it would be almost nine times faster than a sequential implementation.

The matrix multiplier example appears in essentially this form as an example in C.A.R. Hoare, Communicating sequential processes, *Communications of the ACM,* **21** (8) August 1978, pp. 666–677.

7   Parallel sorting

Sorting is a candidate problem for parallel solution because many algorithms have an element of divide-and-conquer. That means the task is carried out by dividing it into some number of smaller, simpler tasks each of which is repeatedly divided until only trivial tasks remain. Such a strategy rapidly identifies independent parts of the original problem, which can be tackled concurrently.

This chapter describes a tree-shaped parallel sorting program, and a way of observing it whilst it is running. I make no claims for the sorting algorithm used, beyond its simplicity, because the real subject is how to observe a parallel program in operation. With very small changes to the sorting program itself, its activity can be displayed on a VDU screen, turning the program into a simulator of its own behaviour.

Sorting strategy

The program consists of a number of simple processes linked together in a tree shaped structure. As in the case of the matrix multiplier, no process need ever know where it is in the tree: there will be only two types of process: leaves, and internal nodes. Again, each process is independent of the size of the problem, and need never store more than two values and some flags, no matter how many values are being sorted. A bigger problem demands a bigger tree, but the components are unchanged.

The strategy is to distribute the numbers upwards from the root of the tree, until they are spread out, one to each leaf. Each process is then responsible for sending back to its parent the sequence of numbers which it has received, but sorted into ascending order. For a leaf, the task is simple, since its one number already constitutes a sequence in ascending order. Each internal node, relying on the sorted subsequences that it will receive from its children, merges two ascending sequences to generate its output sequence.

Each leaf process needs two-way communication with its parent,

```
PROC leaf(CHAN up, down) =
   ...
```

and each internal node needs six channels, two to provide two-way communication with its parent, and two each to and from each of its children.

```
PROC fork(CHAN up, down, left.down, left.up,
                        right.down, right.up) =
   ...
```

For simplicity, the root process is treated as an internal node, with a virtual root process acting as the parent of the root

```
PROC driver(CHAN up.to.tree, down.from.tree) =
   ...
```

and acting as a driver to control the activity of the tree.

To connect these processes, they have to be indexed, so as to correspond to linear arrays of channels. For simplicity, I have made the program a complete balanced tree

```
DEF depth.of.tree = 3 :
```

```
DEF number.of.leaves    = 1 << depth.of.tree ,
    number.of.forks     = number.of.leaves - 1 ,
    number.of.processes = number.of.forks +
                          number.of.leaves ,
    number.of.channels  = number.of.processes :
```

then, numbering the processes breadth-first, upwards from the root

```
DEF root       = 0 ,
    first.fork = root ,
    first.leaf = first.fork + number.of.forks :
```

the children of the internal node process i are indexed $2i + 1$ and $2i + 2$. If channels indexed i are used to connect process i to its parent, these same formulae will give the indexes of the channels to and from the children of internal node process i.

```
CHAN up[number.of.channels], down[number.of.channels] :
PAR
  driver(up[root], down[root])
  PAR i = [first.fork FOR number.of.forks]
    fork(up[i], down[i], down[(2*i)+1], up[(2*i)+1],
                         down[(2*i)+2], up[(2*i)+2])
  PAR i = [first.leaf FOR number.of.leaves]
    leaf(up[i], down[i])
```

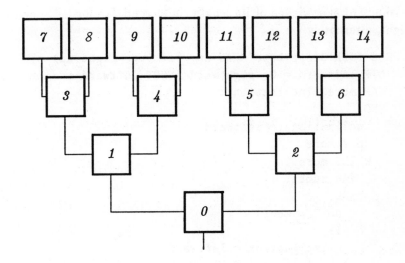

Components of the sorter

There are two phases of activity in the tree: first the sequence of numbers is distributed; then sorted sequences are gathered and merged. Each component process passes through the same two phases.

```
PROC fork(CHAN up, down, left.down, left.up,
                        right.down, right.up) =
  SEQ
    fork.distribute(up, left.up, right.up)
    fork.gather(down, left.down, right.down)  :
```

During the distribution phase, each internal node receives a sequence of numbers from its parent. Notice that since a fork process

knows neither where it is in the tree, nor how big the tree is, it cannot know how many numbers to expect. Accordingly, the sequence is
passed around with each number preceded by a TRUE value, and the
last followed by a FALSE value. Such a sequence can be read by

```
VAR more :
SEQ
  up ? more
  WHILE more
    VAR next :
    up ? next; more
```

The simplest way of distributing the sequence amongst the children,
without foreknowledge of its length, is to send one-for-left, one-for-
right, alternately.

```
PROC fork.distribute(CHAN up, left.up, right.up) =
  DEF leftward = 0, rightward = NOT leftward :
  VAR more, inclination :
  SEQ
    inclination := leftward
    up ? more
    WHILE more
      VAR number :
      SEQ
        up ? number
        IF
          inclination = leftward
            left.up ! TRUE; number
          inclination = rightward
            right.up ! TRUE; number
        up ? more
        inclination := NOT inclination
    PAR
      left.up ! FALSE
      right.up ! FALSE                                          :
```

Notice that this process passes the guarantee of correctly interpolated
TRUE and FALSE values on to its children. Induction from this observation demonstrates that if the root process operates the protocol
correctly, so will each of its descendants.

Since I assumed that the component processes would serve in
an arbitrarily large tree, they should not count the numbers as they

pass upwards. This means that during the merging phase there are again sequences of unknown length to be read, and I will use a similar protocol. The returning sequences of numbers will be coded by preceding each number by a TRUE value, and adding a pair consisting of a FALSE value and a subsequent dummy at the end of the sequence.

In order to do the merging, preserving ordering, numbers must be compared, and this requires that each merging process have at least two registers holding numbers. Since each child sends its sequence in ascending order, the head of each sequence is the minimum of those to come, so the merging process compares the heads, passes on the smaller, and draws one more value from the selected sequence, continuing until the sequences are exhausted.

```
PROC fork.gather(CHAN down, left.down, right.down) =
  VAR left.more,  left.minimum,
      right.more, right.minimum :
  SEQ
    PAR
      left.down ? left.more; left.minimum
      right.down ? right.more; right.minimum
    WHILE left.more OR right.more
      IF
        left.more AND
        ((NOT right.more) OR
                      (left.minimum <= right.minimum))
          SEQ
            down ! TRUE; left.minimum
            left.down ? left.more; left.minimum
        right.more AND
        ((NOT left.more) OR
                      (left.minimum >= right.minimum))
          SEQ
            down ! TRUE; right.minimum
            right.down ? right.more; right.minimum
    down ! FALSE; ANY                                        :
```

Notice a final ANY sent downwards at the end of the sequence, which accounts for the parent process being able to receive a pair of values, ... *more*, ... *minimum*, even when the first is FALSE. This trick is simpler than making the parent's behaviour conditional on the first value, and there is no great cost since after sending down its FALSE value there is nothing left for the child process to do.

The leaf process must be designed to simulate the behaviour of an internal node that only handles a sequence of one number

```
PROC leaf(CHAN up, down) =
  VAR number :
  SEQ
    up ? ANY; number; ANY
    down ! TRUE; number; FALSE; ANY :
```

Finally, the driver process must generate and absorb sequences of numbers, stuffing and stripping the protocol.

```
PROC driver(CHAN up, down) =
  SEQ
    SEQ i = [0 FOR number.of.leaves]
      VAR number :
      SEQ
        ... think of a number
        up ! TRUE; number
    up ! FALSE
    SEQ i = [0 FOR number.of.leaves]
      VAR number :
      SEQ
        down ? ANY; number
        ... do something with the number
    down ? ANY; ANY                            :
```

The missing code controls the behaviour of the whole program. It might, for example, read numbers from the terminal keyboard, and write them back, in ascending order, to the terminal screen.

That completes the sorting program which, whilst it may look overcomplex for a single processor implementation, would look better on an array of *number.of.processes* simple processors. Notice, particularly, that once the numbers have started to emerge from the tree in ascending order, each is available only one comparison time after its predecessor. The advantage would be more obvious were the sorter managing more complex data, where the comparison time might be very large.

Monitoring strategy

The program as it stands can be run on a single processor to simulate the activity of the ideal multi-processor implementation. By writing the missing code in the driver, you could observe numbers going into and coming out of the tree, checking that the program sorts particular sequences of numbers. That tells you nothing about what goes on inside the tree. To get a better idea of *how* the program sorts sequences you might also want to be able to watch the activity in the branches of the tree.

By analogy with the testing of electronic circuits, the idea is to probe the components of the circuit, rather than just watching the signals that pass into and out of the terminals. There are two techniques: breaking connections to measure the current flowing through them corresponds to tapping the channels to watch the traffic; attaching probes to measure the potential at various points in a circuit corresponds to noting the state in each process.

In order to observe the traffic on a channel, a process must be added which duplicates the traffic along a monitoring channel, something like

```
PROC duplicate(CHAN source, sink, copy) =
  WHILE TRUE
    VAR datum :
    SEQ
      source ? datum
      PAR
        copy ! datum
        sink ! datum                          :
```

This process can be inserted into a data stream passing along a channel

```
CHAN channel :
PAR
  producer(channel)
  consumer(channel)
```

allowing the data to be read by another process

```
CHAN channel.a, channel.b, test.data :
PAR
  producer(channel.a)
  duplicate(channel.a, channel.b, test.data)
  consumer(channel.b)
  monitor(test.data)
```

Of course, the observation is not perfect: it may affect the behaviour of the program. First of all, the duplicate process acts as an additional buffer in the data stream. In this example it cannot matter, but were there some other communication, possibly through a third party, between the *producer* and *consumer*, it might matter that the output from the *producer* could proceed, despite the corresponding demand not being made in the *consumer*. Secondly, the *duplicate* process, as written, does not terminate, so unless it is used to observe an infinite data stream, the program will eventually become deadlocked, even had it previously terminated correctly.

In both of these ways you must be careful to design monitoring code that does not interfere excessively with the activity being observed. In general, it is necessary for the behaviour of the monitoring processes to depend on the data passing through them, and this instream technique should be avoided if there are many parallel data paths between pairs of processes in the program being observed.

In order to make internal state visible, it is necessary to add code to the processes being observed. Just as observing traffic involves adding new output processes in parallel with the observed program, so observing state requires that new output processes be set in sequence with the code being observed.

```
PROC p(...) =                   PROC p(..., CHAN test.data) =
  VAR x :                         VAR x :
  SEQ                             SEQ
    .                               .
    .                               .
    .                               .
                                    SEQ
    x := e                            x := e
                                      test.data ! x
    .                               .
    .                               .
    .                               .
                                    SEQ
    c ? x                             c ? x
                                      test.data ! x
    .                               .
    .                               .
    .                               .
```

In order to observe the changing value of a variable each assignment to that variable should be followed by an output process signalling the change on a channel which passes out to the monitoring code. Again, the observation is invasive: you must be aware that the observed process may be delayed by executing the new output processes.

In the example of the parallel sorter, I will use both types of monitoring: the explanation of the behaviour of the merging is in terms of the sequences of values passing along channels, so the traffic along the channels will be watched; the leaves are used as storage locations, so it is appropriate to observe their state.

The result of adding this monitoring code is a number of channels emerging from the tree, each carrying signals indicating the presence or absence of a number. Each will be treated similarly to write a number to, or to remove it from, a position on the screen which will represent the place in the program which is being watched. Since changes to the screen must be made in sequence, it is appropriate to multiplex the test data from the tree, and process each new test signal in sequence.

These decisions lead to the following, changed, program structure

```
DEF number.of.probes = number.of.channels +
                       number.of.leaves :

CHAN up.a[number.of.channels],
     down.a[number.of.channels],
     up.b[number.of.channels],
     down.b[number.of.channels],
     probe[number.of.probes], all.probes  :

PAR
  driver(up.a[root], down.b[root])

  PAR i = [first.fork FOR number.of.forks]
    fork(up.b[i],          down.a[i],
         down.b[(2*i)+1], up.a[(2*i)+1],
         down.b[(2*i)+2], up.a[(2*i)+2])
  PAR i = [first.leaf FOR number.of.leaves]
    leaf(up.b[i], down.a[i],
         probe[number.of.channels + (i - first.leaf)])
  PAR i = [root FOR number.of.channels]
    monitor(up.a[i], down.a[i],
            up.b[i], down.b[i], probe[i])

  multiplex(probe, all.probes)
  display(all.probes, terminal.screen)
```

Each *monitor* process copies data from its ...*a* channels to its ...*b* channels, duplicating the activity along the corresponding *probe*. Every leaf is modified to indicate its state with similar messages. All of these messages are multiplexed onto a single channel, and then translated into sequences of instructions to display the changing state of the program on the terminal screen.

Component processes

There are three types of message to be sent along the *probe* channels: messages indicating the presence of a number, messages indicating the absence of a number, and a final termination message. Each of these will be indicated by starting it with one of three values

```
DEF display.number = 1,
    display.empty  = 2,
    display.stop   = 3 :
```

and the monitoring processes will guarantee that the communications on a *probe* will be a sequence of triples, *display.number* followed by a number followed by a *display.empty*, the whole sequence being followed by a single *display.stop*. Sending an explicit termination signal insulates the monitoring code from changes to the protocol operated in the sorter.

To start with the *leaf* process, all that is needed is to indicate the arrival and departure of the stored number. There are three things which the monitoring code must do: display the number arriving while the tree is filled; clear the display when the number is unloaded; and indicate the end of the leaf's activity.

```
PROC leaf(CHAN up, down, probe) =
  VAR number :
  SEQ
    up ? ANY; number    -- this ANY is TRUE
    probe ! display.number; number
    up ? ANY            -- this one is FALSE

    down ! TRUE; number
    probe ! display.empty
    down ! FALSE; ANY

    probe ! display.stop           :
```

The *monitor* process must copy the sequences of numbers passing first up and then down the tree using the correct protocol for each case. The necessary monitoring code is just what you would need to record changes of state in this buffering processes, so again divides into the same three stages

```
PROC monitor(CHAN up.a, down.a, up.b, down.b, probe) =
  SEQ
    VAR more :
    SEQ
      up.a ? more
      WHILE more
        VAR number :
        SEQ
          up.a ? number
          probe ! display.number; number
          up.b ! more; number
          probe ! display.empty
          up.a ? more
      up.b ! FALSE

    VAR more, number :
    SEQ
      down.a ? more; number
      WHILE more
        SEQ
          probe ! display.number; number
          down.b ! more; number
          probe ! display.empty
          down.a ? more; number
      down.b ! FALSE; ANY

    probe ! display.stop          :
```

Each of the probes coming out of the sorter carries a sequence of display instructions, the last of which is a *display.stop*, so they can all be treated uniformly from now on. The *multiplex* process simply gathers together all of the probe signals, tagging them with the corresponding index number for later identification. Once a *display.stop* is received from a particular probe, no more signals are read from it, and the multiplexer terminates when all probes have been shut off.

```
PROC multiplex(CHAN probe[], all.probes) =
  VAR more, more.from[number.of.probes] :
  SEQ
    more := number.of.probes
    SEQ i = [0 FOR number.of.probes]
      more.from[i] := TRUE

    WHILE more > 0
      VAR instruction :
      ALT i = [0 FOR number.of.probes]
        more.from[i] & probe[i] ? instruction
          IF
            instruction = display.number
              VAR number :
              SEQ
                probe[i] ? number
                all.probes ! instruction; i; number

            instruction = display.empty
              all.probes ! instruction; i

            instruction = display.stop
              SEQ
                more.from[i] := FALSE
                more := more - 1

    all.probes ! display.stop              :
```

Display management

It remains only to translate the stream of probe messages into a
stream of terminal screen control messages. The first thing to do
is to translate the probe numbers into positions on the screen. This
happens in two stages: first the numbers are translated into positions
in a terminal-independent space; then that space is mapped onto the
terminal screen.

```
PROC display(CHAN source, sink) =
  CHAN internal :
  PAR
    independent(source, internal)
    dependent(internal, sink)       :
```

The terminal independent space has right-handed co-ordinates, with the leaves evenly spread across the top, and the root at the middle of the bottom line.

depth.of.tree+2	X	X	X	X		...		X	X	X	X
depth.of.tree+1	X	X	X	X		...		X	X	X	X
depth.of.tree		X		X		...			X		X
$\vdots$											
2					X		...	X			
1						X					

1 2 3 4 5 6 7 ... *number.of.leaves* ...

Messages from probes with index less than *number.of.channels* are from probes within the tree, and those with higher indices are from the leaves. The top line, representing the states of the leaves, is clearly not a part of the pattern in the rest of the tree, so is dealt with differently.

For the internal probes, the simplest solution is to count up from the root. There are $2^{line} - 1$ probes represented on the bottom *line* lines of the display, so the right line for a particular probe is the first for which its index lies below this number. The right column is calculated by discounting the $2^{line-1} - 1$ probes displayed on the lower lines and multiplying by a factor which accounts for the exponentially differing separation of nodes at different depths

```
PROC make.cartesian(VALUE index, VAR x, y) =
  IF
    IF line = [1 FOR depth.of.tree + 1]
      index < ((1 << line) - 1)
        VAR c :
        SEQ
          c := index - ((1 << (line - 1)) - 1)
          x := ((2 * c) + 1) *
                    (number.of.leaves >> (line - 1))
          y := line
    index >= number.of.channels
      SEQ
        x := (2 * (index - number.of.channels)) + 1
        y := depth.of.tree + 2            :
```

The *make.cartesian* process translates a probe index into an x, y pair

$$1 \leq x \leq ((2 \times number.of.channels) - 1)$$
$$1 \leq y \leq depth.of.tree + 1$$

The other terminal independent part of the translation is to turn into digits the numbers that are to be displayed. All the numbers are written in a fixed width field

```
PROC independent(CHAN source, sink) =
  VAR instruction :
  SEQ
    source ? instruction
    WHILE instruction <> display.stop
      SEQ
        sink ! TRUE
        VAR index, x, y :
        SEQ
          source ? index
          make.cartesian(index, x, y)
          sink ! x; y
        IF
          instruction = display.number
            VAR number :
            SEQ
              source ? number
              write.signed(sink, number, field.width)
          instruction = display.empty
            SEQ i = [0 FOR field.width]
              sink ! '*s'
        source ? instruction
    sink ! FALSE                                      :
```

The output from this process consists of a sequence of packets, each beginning with an x, y pair, followed by *field.width* number of characters to be displayed there. Each packet is preceded by a TRUE value, and the whole sequence is terminated with a FALSE.

If the terminal has cursor addressing, then the task is almost complete. Here, for example, is the necessary terminal dependent part of the display process for a *digital VT52* terminal

```
DEF virtual.height = depth.of.tree + 1,
    virtual.width  = (2 * number.of.leaves) - 1 :

PROC dependent(CHAN source, terminal) =
  -- terminal dependent code for driving VT52

  DEF screen.height = 24, screen.width = 80 :
  DEF height.scale = screen.height / virtual.height,
      width.scale  = screen.width / virtual.width :
  DEF control = NOT ((NOT 0) << 5),
      escape = control /\ '[' :
  PROC clear.screen(CHAN terminal) =
    -- clear screen sequence for a VT52
    terminal ! escape ; 'H' ; escape ; 'J'  :
  PROC goto.xy(CHAN terminal, VALUE x, y) =
    -- lefthanded co-ordinates, origin 0,0 at top left
    terminal ! escape ; 'Y' ; '*s' + y ; '*s' + x   :

  VAR more :
  SEQ
    clear.screen(terminal)
    source ? more
    WHILE more
      SEQ
        VAR x, y :
        SEQ
          source ? x; y
          goto.xy(terminal, (x - 1) * width.scale,
                  (virtual.height - y) * height.scale)
        SEQ i = [1 FOR field.width]
          VAR ch :
          SEQ
            source ? ch
            terminal ! ch
        source ? more
    goto.xy(terminal, 0, screen.height - 1)          :
```

The divison of work is such that, if it is at all reasonable to draw
such pictures on a particular terminal, the program can be modified
to do so simply by writing the appropriate *dependent* process. Even
should the terminal not have full cursor control, but only the ability

to move the cursor in small steps, *dependent* can be made to keep
track of the position of the cursor.

For the purpose of the simulator, the simplest coding of the
driver process invents a random sequence of numbers for input to
the tree. A common way of generating an unpredictable sequence of
numbers is to use a linear feedback shift register

```
DEF mask = NOT ((NOT 0) << 9) :

PROC shift(VAR state) =
  SEQ i = [1 FOR 9]
    state := ((state << 1) /\ mask) \/
             (((state >> 4) >< (state >> 8)) /\ 1)  :
```

with an uncontrolled initial state. An arbitrary initial state can be
obtained by reading the real-time clock. Since the shift-register will
not change state if the initial state is all zeroes, the time is ∨-ed with
a one to guarantee a non-zero initial state.

```
PROC driver(CHAN up, down) =
  SEQ
    VAR event, number :
    SEQ
      TIME ? event
      number := (event /\ mask) \/ 1
      SEQ i = [0 FOR number.of.leaves]
        SEQ
          event := event + second
          shift(number)
          up ! TRUE; number
          TIME ? AFTER event
      up ! FALSE
    VAR event :
    SEQ
      TIME ? event
      SEQ i = [0 FOR number.of.leaves]
        SEQ
          event := event + second
          down ? ANY; ANY
          TIME ? AFTER event
          down ? ANY; ANY                          :
```

The driver discards the result of the sort, because all the information has already been displayed, as it passes out of the root process. This coding of the driver pauses after injecting each number into the tree, and after removing each number from the tree, so as to give you time to see what is happening. There is nothing scientific about the choice of a one second pause: I adjusted it to get a satisfactory display from the particular implementation that I was using.

8 Conway's game of Life

Lest you be misled by the name, *Life* is neither a competitive game between several players, nor yet a solitaire game in which a player competes against the collusion between the rules and the roll of the dice. The game is more a simulation, in which the evolution of a system is fully determined by a set of rules.

To be precise, Life is played on an infinite square board: that means that there are a number of squares, or *cells*, each of which has four immediate neighbours and four diagonal neighbours, in the fashion of a chess board. That the board is infinite means simply that every cell in which you will be interested is one with a full complement of neighbours, so that you need never worry about what happens at the edges. There will be only a finite number of interesting cells to think about at any one time. Each cell may be in one of two states: occupied (*alive*) or unoccupied (*dead*), and only finitely many will be alive at any time.

The rules describe the succession of states of each cell in terms of earlier states of that cell and of its eight near neighbours. Each cell passes through a sequence of generations, with the state of the cell in the next generation being determined by its state in this generation, and by the number of cells adjacent to it which are alive in this generation. If a cell is currently alive, and if it has less than two live neighbours, it is deemed to die of loneliness, and will be dead in the next generation. A live cell with two or three neighbours alive in the same generation survives into the next generation, but if it has four or more contemporaries, it will be dead from overcrowding by the next generation. A dead cell with exactly three live neighbours in this generation will give birth and be alive in the next generation,

82

otherwise it will remain barren.

Notice that the rules determine the state of the whole board in the next generation in terms of its state in the present generation. Moreover, the rules are expressed in purely local terms, and the property of Life that makes it interesting is that these local rules can control the evolution of global structures. A number of patterns of live cells are known to pass through cycles of growth and decline, some are known to grow without limit, whilst others die out.

Although the rules of evolution are simple, applying them to a pattern large enough to be interesting, for more than one or two generations, is a tedious business. Machine assistance makes it possible to watch the long term development of substantial colonies, and Life was once a popular way of consuming otherwise unused machine cycles! More practically, a Life board is a particularly simple and symmetrical example of a systolic cellular array. These are studied by VLSI designers seeking algorithms with fast but simple implementations in highly parallel hardware. A systolic array is characterized by the achievement of global co-operation through many simultaneous calculations organized by local communications. Ideally, the components of the array are, like the cells of a Life board, all of a few basic types, have a small finite amount of state, and need never know where they are in the array.

The program described here is, as with the parallel sorter, a simulation in two parts: there is a plane of parallel processes in which the cells of a Life board are represented, one cell to a process; added to this is an essentially sequential mechanism for guiding and watching the evolution of the colony. Perhaps it is worth pointing out at the outset that the resulting program, run on a single processor, is far from the fastest way of playing Life. There are, for example, a number of optimizations that require each process to have a more global view of the state of the board, and naturally give rise to a sequential program. This program is here for two reasons: firstly as an intricate example of the interconnection of processes, showing how to separate this from the workings of the processes themselves; secondly, it is an example of a general method of adding global synchronization to a loosely coupled system in order to observe its behaviour.

The Life board

There is no problem in selecting a representation the board. Each cell of the board has a state, so is represented by a process which administers the variable in which that state is stored. There is no reason why each of these processes should not be identical. Each cell is distinguished only by the particular eight other cells which are close enough to influence its state in the next generation. The neighbours of a cell process are connected to it, each by a pair of channels, one in each direction.

The first problem that arises is one of representing an infinite board on what must necessarily be a finite array of processes. As suggested earlier, the requirement of an infinite board is made so that the behaviour of a cell will not be influenced by its being at an edge of the board. Unless a colony grows without limit, or moves *en masse* in some direction, a finite board will do, since the evolution of a colony is unaffected by any amount of dead space around it.

One solution, and the one that I have adopted here, is to take a finite sized board and wrap it around a torus, so that the cells on the top edge have neighbours on the bottom edge, and those on the right have neighbours on the left.

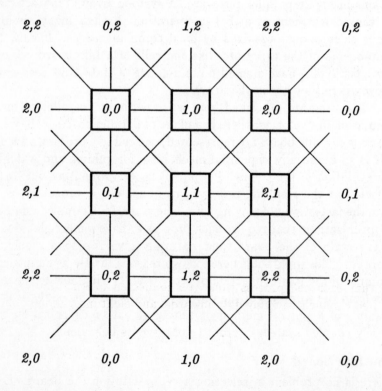

There are now no edges to worry about. You may think of this toroidal board in either of two ways. Looking at it as a flat board with tricky edges, it correctly implements the rules of healthy living until one or more of the edge cells gives birth, from which point on it is possible for things to go wrong, with miraculous conceptions and unexplained deaths happening in ways not predicted by the rules. Another way of thinking about it is that the toroidal board behaves as if it were a fragment of a truly infinite flat board on which the real finite colony that you can see is repeated, in the fashion of a wallpaper pattern, at regular intervals in the horizontal and vertical directions. The boundary effects are now explicable, since they are the effects (predicted by the rules) of a neighbouring copy of the colony coming close enough to influence the visible part of the board.

To be more definite about the program, it consists of a rectangular array of cell processes

```
DEF array.width = ... , array.height = ... :

PAR x = [0 FOR array.width]
  PAR y = [0 FOR array.height]
    ... process representing cell x, y
```

The neighbours of cell x, y are those indexed

$$\langle((x \pm 1) + array.width)\backslash array.width,$$
$$((y \pm 1) + array.height)\backslash array.height\rangle$$

with the remainder operator taking care of the proximity of cells at opposite edges of the board. The numerator of the remainder operator has to be made non-negative, since in *occam* it is defined that the value of $((-1)\backslash w)$ is minus one.

The next thing to decide is the arrangement of the channels connecting these processes. As in the matrix multiplier example, it would be possible to allocate one channel array to account for all of the data flowing in each compass direction. The result would be that each cell process would be connected to eight individually named channels carrying data inwards, and eight individually named channels carrying data outwards. This is to ignore the symmetry with which the rules of living treat the neighbours of a process. A cell does not discriminate between its neighbours according to their compass direction, but treats them uniformly. The symmetry should be represented by a FOR loop in the cell processes, the body being executed eight times, once for each neighbour. That suggests that an array of eight channels is needed, indexed by the eight directions.

Since there are, in *occam*, neither channel variables nor channel pointers, the only neat solution to this problem is to allocate all of the channels from a single large array. Each cell then needs to be told which eight subscripts it should use to select its incoming channels, and which eight to select its outgoing ones.

```
DEF radius      = 1 ,    -- of the 'sphere of influence'
    diameter    = (2 * radius) + 1 ,
    neighbours  = (diameter * diameter) - 1 :

DEF number.of.cells = array.height * array.width,
    number.of.links = neighbours * number.of.cells :

PROC initialize(VALUE x, y, VAR in[], out[]) =
  ... initialize in[...] and out[...]

PROC cell(CHAN link[], VALUE in[], out[]) =
  ... cell using link[in[...]] and link[out[...]]

CHAN link[number.of.links] :
PAR x = [0 FOR array.width]
  PAR y = [0 FOR array.height]
    VAR in[neighbours], out[neighbours] :
      SEQ
        initialize(x, y, in, out)
        cell(link, in, out)
```

Perhaps this is the place to note that I remain unsatisfied by this solution because of the generality of the variable arrays *in*[ ] and *out*[ ]. A mechanical checker, such as might be a part of an *occam* compiler, is unlikely to be able to verify that the *cell* makes only legal use of the *link* channels, since the uses appear to be dynamically determined. A mechanically checkable program would most probably have to recompute the subscripts at the point of use. It is because the effort of recomputing complex subscript expressions would dominate all of the other activity in the program that I have adopted this solution.

The remainder of the board configuration is in the initialization of the indirection arrays, *in*[ ] and *out*[ ]. To do this, an enumeration of the processes and the channels must be chosen. I have chosen to count the processes in the usual way: along the rows then down the colums, from zero at process x zero, y zero in the top left

```
this.process := x + (array.width * y)
```

and to allocate the first eight channels to carry data out of the first process, the next eight out of the next process, and so on. This accounts for all of the channels exactly once, as every channel is outward bound from some process.

To settle on a particular enumeration of channels, the eight neighbours of a process must be put in some order. I choose order of increasing *direction* as computed by the loop

```
SEQ delta.x = [-radius FOR diameter]
  SEQ delta.y = [-radius FOR diameter]
    VAR direction :
    SEQ
      direction := delta.x + (diameter * delta.y)
      ... consider neighbour x+delta.x  y+delta.y
```

which is (except at the top and left edges) the order of increasing process number. The direction of a neighbour characterizes it, and lies in the range

$$-(neighbours/2) \quad \leq \quad direction \quad \leq \quad +(neighbours/2)$$

with the zero value corresponding to the cell at x, y itself. To fill an array with the *neighbour* consecutive subscripts of outward going channels the non-zero values of direction must be mapped onto consecutive indices for *out*, and a group of eight consecutive channel numbers

```
IF
  direction <> 0
    VAR this.index :
    SEQ
      this.index := (neighbours + direction) \
                                      (neighbours + 1)
      out[this.index] := this.index +
                                (neighbours * this.process)
  direction = 0
    SKIP
```

The value of *this.index* constructed in this way ranges from zero to *neighbours* − 1, taking on each value exactly once, in the course of a scan of the neighbours.

Now the question arises of which are the correct subscripts to use to select the incoming links. Incoming links at *this.process* are, if looked at from the other end, the outgoing links from the neighbours of *this.process*.

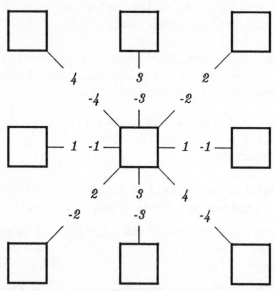

The simplest, brute force, solution to the problem of enumerating them is to put yourself in the position of the process at the other end of each channel, and to ask which link that process would be using to talk to *this.process*, as one of its neighbours. The process at x, y is a neighbour of each of its own neighbours; in particular it is the neighbour in the $-direction$ direction of the process which is its neighbour in the $+direction$ direction. (You can see this because *direction* is linear in *delta.x* and in *delta.y*.) This means that the inward channel from the neighbour in the $+direction$ direction is the one that, at that other process would be described as the outward channel in the $-direction$ direction.

```
SEQ
   other.x := (x + delta.x + array.width)\array.width
   other.y := (y + delta.y + array.height)\array.height
   other.process := other.x + (array.width * other.y)
   other.index   := (neighbours - direction) \
                                          (neighbours + 1)
   in[other.index] := other.index +
                             (neighbours * other.process)
```

I have gathered these fragments in the process *initialize* which appears in the appendix, leaving only the process *cell* to be coded. This is comparatively simple: recording the state of the cell, whether it is *dead* or *alive*, and controlling its evolution

```
DEF dead = 0, alive = NOT dead :

PROC cell(CHAN link[], VALUE in[], out[]) =

  PROC broadcast.present.state(CHAN link[],
                            VALUE out[], state) =
  ... tell neighbours about the state of this cell

  PROC calculate.next.state(CHAN link[],
                VALUE in[], state, VAR next.state) =
  ... evolve in keeping with the rules

  VAR state :
  SEQ
    state := ...                -- set an initial state
    WHILE TRUE
      VAR next.state :
      SEQ
        PAR
          broadcast.present.state(link, out, state)
          calculate.next.state(link,
                            in, state, next.state)
        state := next.state        :
```

I will postpone the matter of what initial value is given to *state*, which determines the type of colony being watched. The second half of this chapter will describe an editor that allows the user to set an initial configuration from the keyboard.

In each generation, each *cell* must learn the state of each of its neighbours. There is a corresponding obligation on a *cell* to tell each of its neighbours about its own current state

```
PROC broadcast.present.state(CHAN link[],
                          VALUE out[], state) =
  PAR i = [0 FOR neighbours]
    link[out[i]] ! state                :
```

To calculate its next state, the *cell* counts the number of adjacent occupied cells, and applies the local rule

```
PROC calculate.next.state(CHAN link[],
                     VALUE in[], state, VAR next.state) =
  VAR count :          -- number of living neighbours
  SEQ
    VAR state.of.neighbour[neighbours] :
    SEQ
      PAR i = [0 FOR neighbours]
        link[in[i]] ? state.of.neighbour[i]
      count := 0
      SEQ i = [0 FOR neighbours]
        IF
          state.of.neighbour[i] = alive
            count := count + 1
          state.of.neighbour[i] = dead
            SKIP
    IF
      count < 2      -- death from isolation
        next.state := dead
      count = 2      -- this cell is stable
        next.state := state
      count = 3      -- stable if alive, a birth if dead
        next.state := alive
      count > 3      -- death from overcrowding
        next.state := dead   :
```

Notice that although the input processes are written in a parallel FOR loop, the counting of live neighbours has to be sequential, since the *count* variable must not be shared. Whilst the simplest of mechanical checkers would be justified in drawing the programmer's attention to the shared array *state.of.neighbour*[ ], it is clear that no element of the array is shared.

Observation and control

As with the parallel sorter, having completed the highly parallel part of the program, I have still to design a means for controlling and watching what happens. The observation will impose more synchronization on the array of cells: there is, so far, nothing to prevent widely separated processes from working on as widely separated generations, but the display should be capable of showing the state of one generation at a time, across the whole of the board.

There are three intructions that the controlling process will need to issue to each cell on the board: it may ask for the cell to assume a new state, so as to initialize, and subsequently edit, the state of the board; it may instruct the cell to evolve for one generation; and it may tell the cell process to terminate.

```
DEF set.state = 1, ask.state = 2, terminate = 3 :
```

In response to instructions to evolve, the cell should yield up its new state. To carry these messages, a channel is needed into each cell, and one from each cell, and the *cell* process must be recoded to expect and comply with the instructions received on its *control* channel:

```
PROC cell(CHAN link[], VALUE in[], out[],
                                CHAN control, sense) =
  VAR state, instruction :
  SEQ
    state := dead     -- the whole board starts off dead
    control ? instruction
    WHILE instruction <> terminate
      SEQ
        IF
          instruction = set.state
            control ? state
          instruction = ask.state
            VAR next.state :
            SEQ
              PAR
                broadcast.present.state(link, out,
                                                state)
                SEQ
                  calculate.next.state(link, in,
                                        state, next.state)
                  sense ! (state <> next.state);
                            next.state
              state := next.state
        control ? instruction                    :
```

This coding of *cell* expects a sequence of instructions, each of which is either a *set.state* followed by a new state to be assumed, or is an

ask.state which causes the cell to evolve and report its new state.
The whole sequence is followed by a single instruction to terminate.
At the end of each generation, the *cell* process sends not only its new
state, but also an indication of whether the state has changed in this
generation. That makes the task of the controlling process simpler.

Since there is only one terminal keyboard and one terminal
screen involved, the controller is essentially a sequential process, with
each of the *control* and *sense* channels connected to it

```
CHAN link[number.of.links],
     control[number.of.cells], sense[number.of.cells] :
PAR
   controller(keyboard, screen, control, sense)
   PAR x = [0 FOR array.width]
     PAR y = [0 FOR array.height]
       VAR in[neighbours], out[neighbours] :
       SEQ
         initialize(x, y, in, out)
         cell(link, in, out, control[x+(array.width*y)],
                             sense  [x+(array.width*y)])
```

The *controller* is written as a state machine, whose state is
changed by characters typed on the keyboard

```
PROC new.activity(VALUE ch, VAR activity) =
... select a new activity
```

Under the control of input from the terminal keyboard, it calls processes either to modify the state of cells on the board by issuing
set.state instructions

```
PROC edit(CHAN keyboard, screen, control[]) =
... modify the colony on the board
```

or to drive the whole board through the evolution of a single generation by scanning the board, issuing *ask.state* instructions, and reading
back the new states.

```
PROC generation(CHAN screen, control[], sense[],
                                        VAR active) =
... cause the colony on the board to move on a step
```

The *active* parameter returns an indication of whether any changes
have happened during the generation.

```
DEF idle              = 1,      editing        = 2,
    single.stepping = 3,      free.running   = 4,
    terminated      = 5 :

PROC controller(CHAN keyboard, screen,
                                control[], sense[]) =
  VAR activity :
  SEQ
    activity := idle
    initialize.display(screen)
    WHILE activity <> terminated
      SEQ
        display.activity(screen, activity)
        VAR ch :
        PRI ALT

          (activity <> editing) & keyboard ? ch
            new.activity(activity, ch)

          (activity = editing) & SKIP
            SEQ
              edit(keyboard, screen, control)
              activity := idle

          (activity = free.running) OR
                  (activity = single.stepping) & SKIP
            VAR changing :
            SEQ
              generation(screen, control,
                                    sense, changing)
              IF
                (activity = single.stepping) OR
                                        (NOT changing)
                    activity := idle
                (activity = free.running) AND changing
                    SKIP

    display.activity(screen, activity)
    SEQ cell = [0 FOR number.of.cells]
      control[cell] ! terminate
    clean.up.display(screen)                          :
```

The normal activity of the controller, *free.running*, is to cause a sequence of invocations of *generation* so that the colony is continually evolving. The alternative has to be asymmetric, because a sequence of calls to *generation* might otherwise go on indefinitely without ever allowing pending keyboard input to be accepted.

Between any two generations, the keyboard has an opportunity to change the activity, by calling *new.activity*

```
PROC new.activity(VAR activity, VALUE ch) =
  -- type 'ch' on the keyboard ...
  IF
    (ch = 'q') OR (ch = 'Q')
                          -- ... Q to finish program
      activity := terminated

    (ch = 's') OR (ch = 'S')
                          -- ... S to halt evolution
      activity := idle

    (ch = 'e') OR (ch = 'E')
                          -- ... E to start editing
      activity := editing

    (ch = 'r') OR (ch = 'R')
                          -- ... R to start evolution
      activity := free.running

    otherwise             -- ... or anything else for
                          --        just one generation
      activity := single.stepping :
```

The *single.step* activity, entered by typing almost anything on the keyboard, causes an evolution of precisely one generation. This makes it easier to follow the details of a history. The code of the board is entirely unaffected by the detailed design of the single stepping mechanism, and even of the details of the editor.

Recall that each cell starts a step of its evolution in response to an *ask.state* instruction, on its *control* channel. It cannot complete the advance unless its neighbours are also on the move, so the *generation* process starts each cell on the board, and then collects a new state from each of the cells.

```
PROC generation(CHAN screen, control[], sense[],
                                        VAR active) =
  SEQ
    SEQ cell = [0 FOR number.of.cells]
      control[cell] ! ask.state
    active := FALSE
    SEQ cell = [0 FOR number.of.cells]
      VAR changed, next.state :
      SEQ
        sense[cell] ? changed; next.state
        IF
          changed
            SEQ
              display.state(screen, cell \ array.width,
                      cell / array.width, next.state)
              active := TRUE
          NOT changed
            SKIP                              :
```

When the new states are gathered, any changes are notified on the
display. A note is also kept of whether *any* of the cells has changed
state, because a colony which does not change in one generation has
become stable, and will never change again. If the colony becomes
stable, the *active* parameter to *generation* is returned as FALSE and
the controller becomes *idle*.

The details of the display are all contained in the process to set
up the screen, to display the state of a cell, to display the activity
of the controller, and to clear up the screen after the program has
terminated. Assuming that the board is some tens of cells on a side,
I have allocated consecutive screen locations to adjacent cells

```
PROC display.state(CHAN screen, VALUE x, y, state) =
  SEQ
    move.cursor(screen, x, y)
    IF
      state = alive
        screen ! '**'
      state = dead
        screen ! '*s'                        :
```

A live cell shows as an asterisk, and a dead cell as a blank space.

To make the initial screen consistent with the initial state of the board, which is entirely dead, it suffices to clear the screen

```
PROC initialize.display(CHAN screen) =
  -- display an entirely dead board
  clear.screen(screen) :
```

and to clean up at the end of the program, the cursor is moved to the left of the line below the image of the board

```
PROC clean.up.display(CHAN screen) =
  move.cursor(screen, 0, array.height)   :
```

Assuming that there is some spare room on the screen to the right of the image of the board, the activity of the controller can be displayed there

```
PROC display.activity(CHAN screen, VALUE activity) =
  SEQ
    move.cursor(screen, array.width+1, array.height/2)
    IF
      activity = idle
        write.string(screen, "Idle")
      activity = editing
        write.string(screen, "Edit")
      activity = single.stepping
        write.string(screen, "Step")
      activity = free.running
        write.string(screen, "Busy")
      activity = terminated
        write.string(screen, "Done")                        :
```

The terminal specific declarations are just those of the process invoked to alter the screen:

```
PROC move.cursor(CHAN screen, VALUE x, y) =
  -- move to column x of line y (of a VT52 screen)
  screen ! escape ; 'Y' ; '*s' + y ; '*s' + x :
```

```
PROC clear.screen(CHAN screen) =
  -- clear the whole of the screen (of a VT52)
  screen ! escape ; 'H' ; escape ; 'J' :
```

All that remains is to supply an editor. Here is a simple process that allows a cursor to be moved around the board image, and allows the state of the cell under the cursor to be set

```
PROC edit(CHAN keyboard, screen, control[]) =

  DEF left.key   = ctrl/\'H',  right.key = ctrl/\'L',
      up.key     = ctrl/\'K',  down.key  = ctrl/\'J',
      uproot.key = '*s',       plant.key = '**'    :

  VAR x, y, editing, ch :
  SEQ
    x := array.width / 2
    y := array.height / 2
    editing := TRUE
    WHILE editing
      SEQ
        move.cursor(screen, x, y)
        keyboard ? ch
        IF
          (ch = left.key) AND (x > 0)
            x := x - 1
          (ch = right.key) AND (x < (array.width - 1))
            x := x + 1
          (ch = up.key) AND (y > 0)
            y := y - 1
          (ch = down.key) AND (y < (array.height - 1))
            y := y + 1
          (ch = uproot.key) OR (ch = plant.key)
            VAR state :
            SEQ
              state := (dead  /\ (ch = uproot.key)) \/
                       (alive /\ (ch = plant.key))
              control[x+(array.width*y)] ! set.state;
                                              state
              display.state(screen, x, y, state)
          (ch = 'q') OR (ch = 'Q')
            editing := FALSE
          otherwise
            SKIP                                      :
```

Editing continues until a character 'Q' is typed. The cursor control keys move the cursor vertically and horizontally over the board, the space bar kills the occupant of a cell, and the asterisk key plants a new occupant. For simplicity, any other character, or an attempt to pass over the boundary of the board image is ignored without comment.

Life

A brief word seems to be in order about the history of *Life* itself. It first became widely known through Martin Gardner's column *Mathematical Games* in the *Scientific American* magazine, in October 1970 (pp. 120–123) and May 1971 (pp. 112–117). The former article explains the rules, and introduces some of the jargon of the subject: for example, the speed of light, which is one cell width per generation, the greatest rate at which information can pass across the board; and the glider, a small, fixed size, moving colony

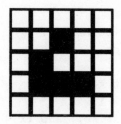

The glider is one of the small, simple colonies whose evolution is fully known: it moves across the board in the direction in which it appears to be pointing, at a quarter of the speed of light, passing through a fixed sequence of four distinct forms.

The second article describes more complicated examples, drawn from the readers' experience of wasting both machine cycles and mathematical ingenuity. Here you will find the curiosities of the subject: Garden of Eden colonies, which are ones that cannot possibly have come about as a result of an evolutionary advance from a former state; the glider gun, a huge structure which grows without limit, by firing an unending stream of gliders from one of its extremities; and a glider-gobbler which, although stable in itself, can also swallow a stream of gliders such as that given off by the gun, to no ill effect. There are viruses, which disrupt regular structures, and regular structures which can recover their symmetry after withstanding a virus attack.

9 Huffman minimum redundancy coding

It has become usual to store data and transmit messages using fixed length codes such as ASCII. The character set is represented by some number of codewords, each of the same length, which in the case of ASCII is seven binary digits. The result is that it takes the same number of bits to store, or the same bandwith to transmit, all messages with the same number of characters. Of course, if you know in advance that your message is in, say, English, then you know that it is much less likely to contain letter 'z's than letter 'e's. This means that if you use a shorter codeword to represent 'e' than that used for 'z', you can expect to use less store, or bandwidth, for the average message.

In ASCII, the message 'easily' is encoded

```
1100101 1100001 1110011 1101001 1101100 1111001
e       a       s       i       l       y
```

requiring forty-two bits, whereas by using a code which included the following representations

$$
\begin{aligned}
a &\mapsto & 1\ 0\ 0\ 1 \\
e &\mapsto & 0 \\
i &\mapsto & 1\ 0\ 1\ 0 \\
l &\mapsto & 1\ 1\ 0\ 0\ 1 \\
s &\mapsto & 1\ 1\ 0\ 1\ 0 \\
y &\mapsto & 1\ 0\ 1\ 1
\end{aligned}
$$

the same message can be encoded

```
0 1 0 0 1 1 1 0 1 0 1 0 1 0 1 1 0 0 1 1 0 1 1
e a     s         i         l         y
```

in only twenty-one bits. The codewords must be chosen in such a way that none is a prefix of any of the others, to ensure that there can be only one way of decoding a particular coded text.

In a classic paper, published in 1952, David Huffman described an algorithm to find the set of codes that would minimize the expected length of a message, given that the probability of each character's occurring were known. Essentially, his method decides the lengths of codewords, giving the longest to the least likely characters. It then remains to create an arbitrary unambiguous code with codewords of the right lengths.

The terminology of Huffman's paper is a little different from that in use today, as indicated in the brackets. He uses the term 'message' to mean an individual character. First of all, the ensemble [= character set] is sorted in decreasing order of probability:

> [It is] necessary that the two least probable messages [= characters] have codes of equal length ... [and that] there be only two of the messages with coded length $L(N)$ which are identical except for their last digits. The final digits of these two codes will be one of the two binary digits, 0 and 1. It will be necessary to assign these two message codes to the Nth and $(N-1)$st messages [= two least probable characters] since at this point it is not known whether or not other codes of length $L(N)$ exist. Once this has been done, these two messages are equivalent to a single composite message. Its code (as yet undetermined) will be the common prefixes of order $L(N)-1$ of these two messages. Its probability will be the sum of the probabilities of the two messages from which it was created. The ensemble containing this composite message in the place of its two component messages will be called the first auxiliary message ensemble.

> This newly created ensemble contains one less message than the original. Its members should be rearranged if necessary so that the messages are again ordered according to their probabilities. It may be considered exactly as the original ensemble was. ...

> This procedure is applied again and again until the number of messages in the most recently formed auxiliary ensemble is reduced to two. One of each of the binary digits is assigned to each of these two composite messages. These messages are then combined to form a single composite mes-

sage with probability unity, and the coding is complete. ...

Having now decided proper lengths of code for each message, the problem of specifying the actual digits remains. Since the combining of messages into their composites is similar to the successive confluences of trickles, rivulets, brooks, and creeks into a final large river, the procedure thus far described might be considered analogous to the placing of signs by a water-borne insect at each of these junctions as he journeys downstream. ...the code we desire is that one which the insect must remember in order to work his way back upstream.

A method for the construction of minimum-redundancy codes, David A. Huffman

in Proc I.R.E., 40 (9), September 1952, pp. 1098-1101

Restated more prosaically, the final paragraph identifies the unambiguous set of codewords with a (binary) tree. Each leaf of the tree corresponds to one of the characters. The depth of that leaf, that is its distance from the root, is the length of that character's codeword. The digits of the codeword are the 'address' of the leaf, that is a sequence of instructions for getting to the leaf from the root, say 0 for 'go to the left' and 1 for 'go to the right'.

Representing a coding tree

As usual, the task of representing a data structure in *occam* amounts to choosing an enumeration for the component parts, so as to map the structure onto a linear array. The structure in question this time is a binary tree similar to that in the sorting example, but this tree may be severely imbalanced, and is of unpredictable depth. This means that the simple fixed enumeration, with the children of node i being nodes $2i + 1$ and $2i + 2$, would be unreasonably wasteful of store, so is unsuitable. A better representation, in this case, roots the tree at node zero

```
DEF root = 0 :
```

and uses an array *eldest*[ ] to record the index of the leftmost offspring of a node, so that the children of node i are indexed *eldest*$[i]$ and *eldest*$[i] + 1$.

Since the root is by definition not the child of any node, the test *eldest*$[node] = root$ can be used to signify that *node* is a leaf of the tree. In the case of the leaves, it will be necessary to know to which character they correspond. This is most readily recorded in another array of the same size as *eldest*[ ] in which the value of *character* [*node*] is the character corresponding to that node, if it is a leaf.

The array *eldest*[ ] makes it easy to pass 'upstream' from the root of the tree to the leaves. In order to make the 'downstream' journey as efficient, it will be useful to record the inverse of *eldest*[ ], in an array *parent*[ ], such that

$$parent\,[eldest\,[node]] = parent\,[eldest\,[node] + 1] = node$$

for each non-leaf node, and the inverse of *character*[ ] in an array *representative*[ ], which records the index of the leaf corresponding to each character.

It remains to be decided how big these arrays must be. This, of course, depends on the size of the character set being encoded. For the purposes of this example, the (unencoded) character set will be signed, eight-bit significant values,

$$-128 \leq ch < 128$$

This allows room for the normal seven-bit characters in the non-negative half range, and room for another, negative, character set which can be used for control information, indicating such things as the end of a message.

```
DEF bits.in.character   = 8,
    number.of.characters = 1 << bits.in.character,
    number.of.codes     = number.of.characters,
    character.mask = NOT((NOT 0)<<bits.in.character) :
```

The *character.mask* has ones as its *bits.in.character* least significant bits, and zeroes elsewhere, for mapping signed characters onto non-negative array indexes, so that, for example,

$$ch = character\,[representative\,[ch \wedge character.mask]]$$

Now if there are *number.of.codes* leaves in a binary tree, then there will be one less than that number of non-leaf nodes, so the total number of nodes is given by

```
DEF size.of.tree = (2 * number.of.codes) - 1 :
```

and the declarations of the arrays for representing the tree are

```
VAR eldest[size.of.tree],
    parent[size.of.tree],
    character[size.of.tree],
    representative[number.of.characters] :
```

Constructing a coding tree

Huffman's algorithm proceeds in two stages. First the character set is sorted into descending order of probability of the character's occurrence. Each of the characters will correspond to a leaf of the tree, so you can think of this stage of the process as constructing *number.of.codes* number of leaves. These leaves will be sub-trees of the final coding tree. Since each is just a leaf, they are disjoint, in the sense that they share no nodes with each other, and they are maximal, in the sense that there is not yet any bigger tree of which any is a member.

The second stage of the algorithm repeatedly reduces the size of the collection of maximal disjoint sub-trees, by combining the two lightest trees to make one new composite tree. By 'lightest' I mean of least *weight* where the weight of a leaf is the probability of the corresponding character, and the weight of a larger tree is the sum of the weights of its leaves. Notice that during this second stage, it is guaranteed that any two siblings—children of a common parent—are already adjacent in descending order of weight. This observation, which I take from Robert Gallager

> A prefix condition code is a code with the property that no codeword is a prefix of any other codeword. A binary tree has the sibling property if each node (except the root) has a sibling, and if the nodes of the tree can be arranged in order of non-increasing probability with each node being adjacent to its sibling. A binary prefix condition code is a Huffman code iff the code tree has the sibling property.
>
> Variations on a Theme by Huffman, Robert G. Gallager
> in IEEE Trans. Information Theory, IT-24(6), 1978, pp. 668-674

is in fact a non-algorithmic characterization of Huffman codes. It also shows that in the representation chosen for the coding tree, which allocates adjacent elements of the arrays to siblings, it is possible to keep the arrays sorted in descending order of weight. Gallager's proof that this property holds is, essentially, an informal proof of correctness of Huffman's algorithm.

Keeping the arrays sorted by weight of node in this way simplifies the finding of the two lightest sub-trees, and if the arrays are filled from the high-index, light, end towards the root, then sub-trees once constructed need not be moved again.

I have divided the algorithm into three parts

PO-H

```
PROC construct.tree(VALUE probability[]) =
  VAR left.limit, right.limit, weight[size.of.tree] :

  PROC construct.leaves =
  ... build the leaves of the tree

  PROC construct.other.nodes =
  ... join pairs of subtrees until only one remains

  PROC invert.representation =
  ... set parent[] and representative[]

  SEQ
    left.limit    := size.of.tree + 1
    right.limit   := size.of.tree + 1

    -- left.limit = (size.of.tree + 1)
    -- (right.limit - left.limit) = 0

    construct.leaves

    -- left.limit = number.of.codes
    -- (right.limit - left.limit) = number.of.codes

    construct.other.nodes

    -- left.limit = root
    -- (right.limit - left.limit) = 1

    invert.representation      :
```

Throughout, the collection of maximal disjoint sub-trees consists of those trees rooted at nodes for which

$$left.limit \leq node < right.limit$$

The initialization of the limits makes this collection empty. The process *construct.leaves* introduces a new sub-tree into the collection for each of the characters of the character set, setting its weight according to the probability of the character, maintaining the arrangement of the leaves in descending order, so that

$$left.limit \leq i \leq j < size.of.tree \quad \Longrightarrow \quad weight[i] \geq weight[j]$$

The process *construct.other.nodes* combines the two lightest leaves, which are those nearest to *right.limit*. It introduces a new node with the combined weight of these two, adjusting the limits of the collection, and filling in the shape of the tree in *eldest*[ ]. Finally, the process *invert.representation* constructs the arrays *parent*[ ] and *representative*[ ].

Both *construct.leaves* and *construct.other.nodes* repeatedly create a new node of some given weight, and insert it into the right place between the limits to maintain the weight ordering of the nodes. The determination of this right place, and the consequent adjustment of the lighter nodes is done by

```
PROC insert.new.node( VAR new.node,
                      VALUE weight.of.new.node,
                      VAR left.limit,
                      VALUE right.limit ) =
  VAR weight.limit :
  SEQ
    IF
      IF node = [left.limit FOR right.limit-left.limit]
        weight[node] <= weight.of.new.node
          weight.limit := node
      TRUE
        weight.limit := right.limit
    SEQ node = [left.limit FOR weight.limit-left.limit]
      SEQ
        character[node - 1] := character[node]
        eldest[node - 1]    := eldest[node]
        weight[node - 1]    := weight[node]
    left.limit          := left.limit - 1
    new.node            := weight.limit - 1
    weight[new.node] := weight.of.new.node       :
```

Recall that the collection of maximal disjoint sub-trees of the coding tree so far constructed consists of those rooted at nodes

$$left.limit \leq node < right.limit$$

and that they are in descending order of weight. This means that the conditional sets the *weight.limit* so that

$$left.limit \leq node < weight.limit \implies$$
$$weight[node] > weight.of.new.node$$
$$weight.limit \leq node < right.limit \implies$$
$$weight.of.new.node \geq weight[node]$$

The sequential loop then displaces each of the heavier nodes one place to the left to make room for the *new.node*, and the *left.limit* of the collection is adjusted to compensate. The shapes of the sub-trees remain the same, so apart from being shifted up by one no changes are necessary to the value in *eldest*[ ]. This is because only nodes to the left of the *weight.limit* are moved, but

$$node < weight.limit \implies node < right.limit$$

and the construction guarantees

$$(eldest[node] = root) \lor (eldest[node] \geq right.limit)$$

so that no node which is moved is yet a child.

Using this process, *insert.new.node*, the process that creates the leaf nodes can be written

```
PROC construct.leaves =
  DEF minimum.character = -(number.of.characters / 2) :
  SEQ ch = [minimum.character FOR number.of.characters]
    VAR new.node :
    SEQ
      insert.new.node(new.node,
                probability[ch /\ character.mask],
                left.limit, right.limit)
      eldest[new.node]    := root
      character[new.node] := ch                        :
```

This inserts a new leaf into the collection, increasing the size of the collection by decreasing the *left.limit*. The process to combine the leaves into a tree

```
PROC construct.other.nodes =
  WHILE (right.limit - left.limit) <> 1
    VAR new.node :
    SEQ
      right.limit := right.limit - 2
      insert.new.node(new.node,
            weight[right.limit] + weight[right.limit+1],
            left.limit, right.limit)
      eldest[new.node] := right.limit        :
```

first removes the two lightest sub-trees from the collection, by decreasing *right.limit*, then joins them under a parent whose weight is the sum of their individual weights. Notice that the assignment to *eldest[new.node]* maintains the property that there are no children to the left of the *right.limit*. The process is complete when only one tree remains.

Inverting the representation of the tree is a simple task, which involves assigning to *representative[ ]* the indexes of the leaf nodes, and to *parent[ ]* the indexes of the nodes that are not leaves, thus

```
PROC invert.representation =
  SEQ node = [root FOR size.of.tree]
    IF
      eldest[node] = root
        representative[character[node] /\
                              character.mask] := node
      eldest[node] <> root
        SEQ child = [eldest[node] FOR 2]
          parent[child] := node                :
```

That completes the code to construct a coding tree from a given probablity distribution.

Encoding and decoding using a coding tree

The encoding of any given character *ch* is the sequence of 'go left' and 'go right' instructions that Huffman's insect must follow to pass upstream from the root node to the representative node of that character. It is easy enough to construct this code backwards, since floating downstream involved passing from *node* to *parent[node]* in succession from the representative node until the root is reached. The process

```
SEQ
  length := 0
  node := representative[ch /\ character.mask]
  WHILE node <> root
    SEQ
      encoding[length] := node - eldest[parent[node]]
      length          := length + 1
      node            := parent[node]
```

establishes the condition that

$$\bigwedge_{0 \leq i < length} node_i = (eldest[node_{i+1}] + encoding[i])$$

where

$$node_0 = representative[ch \wedge character.mask]$$
$$node_{length} = root$$

so that the encoding of *ch* can be transmitted in the right order by

```
SEQ i = [1 FOR length]
  output ! encoding[length - i]
```

It remains only to decide how much room needs to be allocated to store the *encoding*[ ] whilst it is being constructed. Assume that you are decoding a Huffman encoded character. Before you receive the first bit of the encoding, there are *number.of.codes* possible codes that you might be about to receive. Each bit that you receive divides the set of possible characters into two non-empty sub-sets: those that are still possible, and those that are now precluded. This means that at most *number.of.codes* − 1 bits will suffice. In fact, in the worst case, this limit is achieved: if each character is more than twice as probable as the next most likely, then the Huffman codes are, in decreasing order of probability

$$0, \quad 10, \quad 110, \quad 1110, \quad 11110, \quad \ldots$$

with the two least probable characters both having encodings that are *number.of.codes* − 1 bits long. With this knowledge, the encoding process is written

```
PROC encode.character(CHAN output, VALUE ch) =
  -- Transmit the encoding of ch along output
  DEF size.of.encoding = number.of.codes - 1 :
  VAR encoding[size.of.encoding], length, node :
  SEQ
    length := 0
    node    := representative[ch /\ character.mask]
    WHILE node <> root
      SEQ
        encoding[length] := node - eldest[parent[node]]
        length := length + 1
        node    := parent[node]
    SEQ i = [1 FOR length]
      output ! encoding[length - i]                    :
```

Decoding a stream of bits to determine the character consists of following the 'go left' and 'go right' instructions as they arrive

```
SEQ
  input ? bit
  node := eldest[node] + bit
```

Enough bits must be accepted to pass 'upstream', starting from the root node until a leaf is reached. That leaf indicates the decoded character

```
PROC decode.character(CHAN input, VAR ch) =
  VAR node :
  SEQ
    node := root
    WHILE eldest[node] <> root
      VAR bit :
      SEQ
        input ? bit
        node := eldest[node] + bit
    ch := character[node]                    :
```

Having once fixed on a coding tree, the encoding process can be applied repeatedly to a sequence of characters to produce a sequence of bits which, by repeated application of the decoding process, can be turned back into the original sequence of characters. In this way, you can code a pair of processes that when executed in parallel duplicate the behaviour of a buffer like *copy*:

```
PROC copy(CHAN source, end.of.source, sink) =
  -- Copy characters from source to sink until a
  -- signal is received from end.of.source
  VAR more.characters.expected :
  SEQ
    more.characters.expected := TRUE
    WHILE more.characters.expected
      VAR ch :
      ALT
        source ? ch
          sink ! ch
        end.of.source ? ANY
          more.characters.expected := FALSE :
```

transmitting the minimum number of bits necessary to communicate
the information in the sequence of characters.

I will assume that the probabilities of the characters are fixed in
advance, perhaps by considering an average over many messages of
the type to be sent.

```
DEF probability = TABLE[ ... ] :
            -- indexed by [0 FOR number.of.characters]
```

In order to keep all the arithmetic in integers, the probabilities should
be scaled and rounded so that the total of the 'probabilities'

$$\sum_{ch} probability\,[ch]$$

is a large integer. If it is possible to read the message through before
sending it, then you can count actual character frequencies, and produce an optimal Huffman code for the message, but of course you will
then have to transmit a description of the code with your message!

If one of the character codes is laid aside to indicate the end of
a transmission,

```
DEF end.of.message = -1 :
```

then that can be transmitted after the last real character of the message. That means that the end of the message is marked within the
sequence of Huffman encodings of the characters.

The process

```
PROC copy.encoding(CHAN source, end.of.source, sink) =
  -- Read characters from source, sending their
  -- encodings along sink, until a signal is received
  -- along end.of.source.
  VAR more.characters.expected :
  SEQ
    construct.tree(probability)
    more.characters.expected := TRUE
    WHILE more.characters.expected
      VAR ch :
      ALT
        source ? ch
          encode.character(sink, ch)
        end.of.source ? ANY
          more.characters.expected := FALSE
      encode.character(sink, end.of.message)        :
```

translates a stream of characters into a stream of bits representing
their Huffman encodings, and marks the end of the stream by sending
the encoding of *end.of.message*. The corresponding decoding process
would be

```
PROC copy.decoding(CHAN source, sink) =
  -- Read a bit stream from source, decoding it into
  -- characters and send these along sink until
  -- end.of.message is decoded
  VAR more.characters.expected :
  SEQ
    construct.tree(probability)
    more.characters.expected := TRUE
    WHILE more.characters.expected
      VAR ch :
      SEQ
        decode.character(source, ch)
        IF
          ch <> end.of.message
            sink ! ch
          ch = end.of.message
            more.characters.expected := FALSE    :
```

These processes can be used at the opposite ends of a serial communications medium

```
PROC copy.over.serial.medium(CHAN source,
                             end.of.source, sink) =
  -- Copy characters from source to sink until a
  -- signal is received from end.of.source
  DEF end.of.message = -1,
      probability = TABLE[ ... ] :
  CHAN serial.medium :
  PAR
    copy.encoding(source, end.of.source, serial.medium)
    copy.decoding(serial.medium, sink)                  :
```

where each communication on *serial.medium* is the transmission of
a single bit. The process *copy.over.serial.medium* is a buffer: provided a sequence of bytes is communicated on *source* which does not
include *end.of.message* (if for example they are all seven-bit character codes) either *copy* or *copy.over.serial.medium* can be substituted
for the other in any program without affecting the behaviour of the
program.

Many communications media are most efficiently used by sending
fixed sized messages, consisting of large numbers of bits. You already
have most of the components necessary to implement a process like
copy which makes efficient use of such a medium. Encoding characters and packing the bits into blocks can be done by *copy.encoding*
executing concurrently with *pack.bits.into.blocks* from an earlier section.

```
PROC encode.into.blocks(CHAN source, end.of.source,
                                     block.sink) =
  CHAN bit.stream, end.of.bit.stream :
  PAR
    SEQ
      copy.encoding(source, end.of.source, bit.stream)
      end.of.bit.stream ! ANY
    pack.bits.into.blocks(bit.stream,
                          end.of.bit.stream, block,sink) :
```

Decoding the characters from the stream of blocks is a slightly
trickier task, since the end of the message is determined from the decoded data. The most elegant solution, as seems common in parallel
programs, involves a process that throws away unwanted information

```
PROC discard(CHAN source, end.of.source) =
  VAR more.expected :
  SEQ
    more.expected := TRUE
    WHILE more.expected
      ALT
        source ? ANY
          SKIP
        end.of.source ? ANY
          more.expected := FALSE      :
```

This inputs successively from *source*, ignoring the values that it receives, until a signal is sent to it on *end.of.source*. With this, the process for decoding the bits in a stream of blocks can be written

```
PROC decode.from.blocks(CHAN block.source, sink) =
  CHAN end.of.block.source,
       bit.stream, end.of.bit.stream :
  PAR
    SEQ
      unpack.bits.from.blocks(block.source,
                      end.of.block.source, bit.stream)
      end.of.bit.stream ! ANY        -- 'feed-forward'

    SEQ
      copy.decoding(bit.stream, sink)
      PAR
        discard(bit.stream, end.of.bit.stream)
        end.of.block.source ! ANY  :  -- 'feed-back'
```

When *copy.decoding* decodes an *end.of.message* it terminates, causing a signal to be offered for output on *end.of.block.stream*, which is a feed-back path to the block unpacking process. At the same time, *discard* absorbs any bits that were left in the last block of the message. When all of the bits of the last block have gone, *unpack.bits.from.blocks* accepts the *end.of.block.source* signal, and terminates, causing an *end.of.bit.stream* signal to be sent to terminate the *discard* process.

These two processes can be operated concurrently to simulate a buffer

```
PROC copy.over.blocked.medium(CHAN source,
                              end.of.source, sink) =
-- Copy characters from source to sink until a
-- signal is received from end.of.source
DEF end.of.message = -1,
    probability = TABLE[ ... ] :
CHAN blocked.medium :
PAR
  encode.into.blocks(source, end.of.source,
                                 blocked.medium)
  decode.from.blocks(blocked.medium, sink)          :
```

with each communication on the *blocked.medium* being a transfer of
a block of the predetermined fixed size.

The *copy.over.blocked.medium* is not quite as good an implementation of a buffer as is the bit-serial copy. Consider what communications must happen before the first character is output on *sink*. This
is a restriction on the contexts in which *copy.over.blocked.medium*
can be substituted for *copy*.

Adapting the code to the message

So far, I have accepted Huffman's assumption that the code is predetermined and remains fixed throughout the transmission of a given
message. This is reasonable in case the probability distribution of the
characters in the message is known in advance, or if the message can
be read through in advance. Gallager suggests an alternative encoding that tends in the long run towards the fixed Huffman encoding,
but which starts with no knowledge of the probability distribution of
the characters, adapting the code as the message is being sent.

Each character is encoded with a Huffman code that would be
optimal for a message consisting of all those characters that have gone
before it. This encoding technique has the startling property that,
since the decoder has already decoded the preceding characters, it can
deduce from the received message what code should be used to decode
each character. There is no longer a problem in communicating the
code as well as the message!

As I have presented it, it might seem that Gallager's adaptive
Huffman coder requires that a new coding tree be constructed for
each character of the transmitted and received message. Fortunately,
this is not the case: the accumulated character frequencies change
little, so the shape of the tree tends to settle down; successive trees

are sufficiently similar that it is fairly easy to construct each from its predecessor.

The idea is to write a process *increment.frequency*(*ch*) which modifies the coding tree so as to be consistent with a frequency distribution with one more occurrence of the character *ch* than previously. The encoding process becomes

```
PROC copy.encoding(CHAN source, end.of.source, sink) =
  VAR more.characters.expected :
  SEQ
    construct.tree
    more.characters.expected := TRUE
    WHILE more.characters.expected
      VAR ch :
      ALT
        source ? ch
          SEQ
            encode.character(sink, ch)
            increment.frequency(ch)
        end.of.source ? ANY
          more.characters.expected := FALSE
    encode.character(sink, end.of.message)            :
```

and the corresponding decoding process would be

```
PROC copy.decoding(CHAN source, sink) =
  VAR more.characters.expected :
  SEQ
    construct.tree
    more.characters.expected := TRUE
    WHILE more.characters.expected
      VAR ch :
      SEQ
        decode.character(source, ch)
        IF
          ch <> end.of.message
            SEQ
              sink ! ch
              increment.frequency(ch)
          ch = end.of.message
            more.characters.expected := FALSE    :
```

To keep track of the accumulated frequencies, the *weight*[ ] must become a permanent part of the representation of the tree

```
VAR weight[size.of.tree] :
```

In order to increment the recorded frequency of a character, it is necessary to increment the weight of its representative leaf

```
VAR node :
SEQ
  node := representative[ch /\ character.mask]
  weight[node] := weight[node] + 1
```

There are two ways in which this may have damaged the structure of the tree. First of all, unless the tree has only the one node, the weight of the parent of node is no longer the sum of the weights of its children: it will be necessary to increment the weights of the parent of the node, and all of its ancestors up to the root

```
VAR node :
SEQ
  node := representative[ch /\ character.mask]
  WHILE node <> root
    SEQ
      weight[node] := weight[node] + 1
      node := parent[node]
  weight[root] := weight[root] + 1
```

Secondly, each time the weight of a node, be that the original leaf or one of its ancestors, is increased there is a danger that the ordering of the weights may be upset. If this is the case then it is time to reorganize the tree, and change the encoding.

Assuming that the tree is initially properly ordered, then the ordering will first fail when $weight[node - 1] = weight[node]$ and the weight of *node* is about to be incremented. Now, the trees rooted at nodes of equal weight must be disjoint trees, that is either the nodes are siblings, or they have ancestors which are siblings. This follows from the fact that the weight of a node is always less than that of its ancestors, and greater than that of its descendants, so another node with the same weight is neither an ancestor nor a descendant.

To preserve the ordering on the nodes, it would be possible to exchange the trees rooted at *node* and *node − 1*, and then to increment the weight of the light node in its new position. Since there might be many nodes with the same weight, however, this would have to be done repeatedly, shuffling the imminently overweight node leftwards in the tree.

```
WHILE weight[node-1] = weight[node]
  SEQ
    swap.trees(node, node - 1)
    node := node - 1
```

An alternative solution is to look for the leftmost node of the given weight, and exchange with that node, directly. The same argument about the weight of a node being less than that of its ancestors shows that there is always a sequence of nodes for which

$$weight[(node - i) - 1] > weight[node - i] = \ldots = weight[node]$$

This leftmost node, indexed $node - i$, is identified, and the exchange performed, by

```
IF i = [1 FOR (node - root) - 1]
  weight[(node - i) - 1] > weight[node]
    SEQ
      swap.trees(node, node - i)
      node := node - i
```

Having moved the node, it is possible to increment its weight, and that of each of its ancestors.

```
VAR node :
SEQ
  node := representative[ch /\ character.mask]
  WHILE node <> root
    IF
      weight[node-1] > weight[node]
        SEQ
          weight[node] := weight[node] + 1
          node := parent[node]
      weight[node-1] = weight[node]
        IF i = [1 FOR (node - root) - 1]
          weight[(node - i) - 1] > weight[node]
            SEQ
              swap.trees(node, node - i)
              node := node - i
              weight[root] := weight[root] + 1
```

The process for exchanging a pair of disjoint sub-trees is simply coded

```
PROC swap.trees(VALUE i, j) =
  -- Exchange disjoint sub-trees rooted at i and j

  PROC swap.words(VAR p, q) =
    -- Exchange values stored in p and q
    VAR t :
    SEQ
      t := p
      p := q
      q := t           :

  PROC adjust.offspring(VALUE i) =
    -- Restore downstream pointers to node i
    IF
      eldest[i] = root
        representative[character[i]/\character.mask]:=i
      eldest[i] <> root
        SEQ child = [eldest[i] FOR 2]
          parent[child] := i                          :

  SEQ
    swap.words(eldest[i], eldest[j])
    swap.words(character[i], character[j])
    adjust.offspring(i)
    adjust.offspring(j)                               :
```

First, the 'upstream' pointers, *eldest*[ ] and *character*[ ], to the nodes are exchanged, then the process *adjust.offspring* restores the 'downstream' pointers that are no longer correct. There is, of course, no need to exchange the weights of the nodes, since they were known to be equal.

The only remaining problem is to decide the shape of the initial coding tree: what encoding should be used to send the first character? The simplest solution would be to construct the initial tree on the assumption that all characters are equally likely to turn up, say

$$eldest[node] = root \implies weight[node] = 1$$

This means that, to begin with, the code is a fixed length one, each character being encoded by *bits.in.character* number of bits.

An alternative technique is to keep in the coding tree only representations of characters that have actually been sent and received. Whenever a character is to be sent for the first time in the message, the code of a special escape 'character' is sent, followed by some standard representation of the new character, say its ASCII code. A new leaf must then be added to the tree to represent the new character.

In order to accommodate the escape character, the space allocated for the tree must be enlarged

```
DEF number.of.codes = number.of.characters + 1 :
```

and, since the tree grows, some way must be found of recording that size. As each escape is the representation of a character that has never occurred at all (you may not yet know which character, but you do know this), it should be given a very low weight. This means that it is reasonable to represent it by the rightmost (least likely) leaf of the tree. Doing this means that a single variable

```
VAR escape :
```

serves the purpose of recording which node represents the escape, and which is the rightmost node of the tree.

Since the value of *escape* changes, it will not do to use it as an initial value for *representative*[ ]. Define, instead,

```
DEF not.a.node = size.of.tree :
```

then creating the initial tree is just a matter of making the escape leaf, and initializing the array of representatives

```
PROC construct.tree =
  SEQ
    escape := root
    weight[escape] := 1      -- minimum legal weight
    eldest[escape] := root  -- it is a leaf
    SEQ ch = [0 FOR number.of.characters]
      representative[ch] := not.a.node            :
```

Encoding using the new tree is substantially unchanged, excepting in that some provision must be made for sending escaped characters. First of all, the encoding is potentially larger by the *bits.in.character* number of bits in the unencoded representation, so

```
DEF size.of.encoding = bits.in.character +
                       (number.of.codes - 1)   :
```

The bits of the unencoded character representation can then be stored before the encoding of escape, to be transmitted after it.

```
SEQ i = [0 FOR bits.in.character]
  encoding[i] := (ch >> i) /\ 1
```

The encoding of the escape changes as the tree is modified. It is of course to be found by applying the same algorithm to the node representative of escape, as would be applied to the representative of any character.

```
PROC encode.character(CHAN output, VALUE ch) =
  -- Transmit the encoding of ch along output
  DEF size.of.encoding = bits.in.character +
                          (number.of.codes - 1)   :
  VAR encoding[size.of.encoding], length, node :
  SEQ
    IF
      representative[ch/\character.mask] <> not.a.node
        SEQ
          length := 0
          node   := representative[ch/\character.mask]
      representative[ch/\character.mask] = not.a.node
        SEQ
          SEQ i = [0 FOR bits.in.character]
            encoding[i] := (ch >> i) /\ 1
                            -- i'th bit of unencoded ch
          length := bits.in.character
          node   := escape
    WHILE node <> root
      SEQ
        encoding[length] := node - eldest[parent[node]]
        length := length + 1
        node   := parent[node]
    SEQ i = [1 FOR length]
      output ! encoding[length - i]                    :
```

The very first character to be sent will be escaped, and since the representative node for *escape* is initially *root* the encoding of the escape will be the null sequence of bits. This means that the first transmitted bit will be the first bit of the unencoded character representation.

Decoding is also similar to decoding with a fixed code, excepting that on receipt of the encoding of escape, the bits of the unencoded escaped character must be read and the character reassembled.

The first bit of an escaped sequence is the sign bit of the character code, which the assignment

```
SEQ
  input ? bit
  ch := - bit
```

extends to the left, and subsequent bits can be shifted in from the right.

In any case, the first action is to accept enough bits to represent a leaf node: initially a sequence of no bits is enough to represent the only leaf, which is *escape*. Then, if the leaf represents a character, that character has been decoded; if the leaf represents the escape, the character code is reconstructed

```
PROC decode.character(CHAN input, VAR ch) =
  -- Receive an encoding along input and store the
  -- corresponding character in ch
  VAR node :
  SEQ
    node := root
    WHILE eldest[node] <> root
      VAR bit :
      SEQ
        input ? bit
        node := eldest[node] + bit
    IF
      node < escape
        ch := character[node]
      node = escape
        VAR bit :          -- read signed character code
        SEQ
          input ? bit
          ch := - bit
          SEQ i = [2 FOR bits.in.character - 1]
            SEQ
              input ? bit
              ch := (ch << 1)  bit            :
```

In order to increment the frequency of a character not yet in the tree, it is necessary to be able to construct a new leaf to be the representative of the new character. The new character has never previously been received, so its initial weight should be as low as possible, which means that it belongs next to the *escape* node, at the low-probability end of the tree.

The simplest way of adding a node to the tree is to create a node of zero weight, and then increment its weight (to one) exactly as though it had previously existed. This process divides the escape leaf into three: two new leaves and their parent

```
PROC create.leaf(VAR new.leaf, VALUE ch) =
   -- Extend the tree by fision of the escape leaf
   -- into two new leaves
   VAR new.escape :
   SEQ
     new.leaf              := escape + 1
     new.escape            := escape + 2

     eldest[escape]        := new.leaf
                        -- the old escape is the new parent

     weight[new.leaf]      := 0
     eldest[new.leaf]      := root
     parent[new.leaf]      := escape
     character[new.leaf] := ch
     representative[ch /\ character.mask] := new.leaf

     weight[new.esape]     := 1
     eldest[new.escape]    := root
     parent[new.escape]    := escape

     escape                := new.escape                    :
```

The new leaf has no weight when created, so there is no effect on the weights of its ancestors. Notice that a brand new leaf having no weight, the earlier data invariant—that no node has the same weight as its parent—is breached by the *escape* node and its parent. This invariant was used to show that the sub-tree exchanging was correct, so that argument has to be re-constructed. The statement of the invariant must be strengthened: no node, excepting the *escape* node has the same weight as its parent. This is sufficient (as you should check) because it is never required that the one-node tree rooted at *escape* be exchanged with any other (why not?).

Creating a new representative with zero weight makes new characters like those already present in the tree. In either case, recording the arrival of a character is a matter of finding a representative leaf for it, and then incrementing the weight of that leaf and making the consequential adjustments to the tree.

```
PROC increment.frequency(VALUE ch) =
  VAR node :
  SEQ
    IF
      representative[ch/\character.mask] <> not.a.node
        node := representative[ch /\ character.mask]
      representative[ch/\character.mask] = not.a.node
        create.leaf(node, ch)
    WHILE node <> root
      IF
        weight[node-1] > weight[node]
          SEQ
            weight[node] := weight[node] + 1
            node := parent[node]
        weight[node-1] = weight[node]
          IF i = [1 FOR (node - root) - 1]
            weight[(node - i) - 1] > weight[node]
              SEQ
                swap.trees(node, node - i)
                node := node - i
    weight[root] := weight[root] + 1                    :
```

That completes the adaptive coder. Notice that, since the processes *copy.encoding* and *copy.decoding* have the same interfaces as the corresponding processes in the fixed-code coder, they may be substituted into the example *copy...* processes. There is no need to change the processes that convey the bit stream from encoder to decoder.

10 The occam notation

This section contains a summary of the programming language, based on that in INMOS's *occam Programming Manual* (Prentice-Hall International, 1984). It codifies the language used in this book, which matches neither any implementation known to me, nor (in every detail) any other documentation. I have followed the definition in the *Programming Manual* except where the baroqueness of the quirks in the language that it describes suggest error rather than intention.

Micro-syntax and layout

The layout of an *occam* program is significant in a way unusual in a modern programming language. A program is written as a sequence of *logical lines*, each line preceded by an indentation the depth of which is significant to the structure of the program.

A logical line can be broken into several *physical lines* by breaking it after a binary operator, comma, semicolon or ampersand. The indentation of the logical line is the number of leading spaces on its first physical line, and each of its physical lines must begin with at least this many spaces.

A physical line ends at an end-of-line, or at the first occurrence of two consecutive minus signs, which introduce a comment that extends to the end-of-line. Within a physical line, spaces are significant only between quotes, or where they separate two words or numbers that might otherwise form a single word or number, or two symbols that might be a single symbol.

A *name* is a sequence of letters and digits and full-stops, the first of which is a letter. Two names are different unless they are the same sequences of characters. The following sequences are not names, but are reserved as symbols

AFTER	CONST	PAR	TABLE
ALT	DEF	PLACED	TIME
AND	FALSE	PRI	TRUE
ANY	FOR	PROC	VALUE
AT	IF	SEQ	VAR
BYTE	NOT	SKIP	WHILE
CHAN	OR	STOP	

A sequence of decimal digits is a *numeral*, whose value is the corresponding non-negative integer. A sequence of decimal digits preceded by a sign is a *signednumeral*, whose value is the corresponding integer. In either case, the twos-complement representation of the integer must fit into the word of the implementing machine.

A hash sign, '#', followed by a sequence of hexadecimal digits is a *numeral* whose value is the corresponding bit pattern, adjusted to the word size of the implementing machine by adding or removing zeroes at the left. The case of the letters in a hexadecimal numeral is insignificant.

A *character denotation* between a pair of single quotes is also a numeral. Except for the single quote, double quote and asterisk characters, any printable ASCII character, that is one with a code greater than 31_{10} and less than 127_{10}, is a character denotation, whose value is the corresponding code. The following are also character denotations, whose values are the codes of these characters

*c or *C	carriage return	(13_{10})
*n or *N	new line	(10_{10})
*s or *S	space	(32_{10})
*t or *T	horizontal tab	(9_{10})
*'	single quote	(39_{10})
*"	double quote	(34_{10})
**	asterisk	(42_{10})

Any number between zero and 255_{10} also has a corresponding character denotation consisting of an asterisk, followed by a hash sign and two hexadecimal digits.

A (possibly empty) sequence of no more than 255_{10} character denotations between a pair of double quotes is an abbreviation for a *table* of BYTE expressions. The value of the first byte of the table is the number of character denotations, and the remaining bytes are the values of the character denotations in sequence.

Notation

The syntax is described by productions in a BNF modified to cope with the two-dimensional syntax of *occam*. Items enclosed in rectangular boxes represent literal text, and words in italics represent syntactic categories. The production

$$repetition = \boxed{\text{WHILE}}\ expression$$
$$process$$

means that a *repetition* consists of the word WHILE followed on the same line by an *expression*, with a *process* below it and indented two columns further than the keyword. Vertical bars separate alternative decompositions of classes, brackets surround optional parts, and braces parts which may be omitted or repeated any number of times. For example, the productions

$$expr = atom\ [\boxed{-}\ atom]\ \big|\ atom\ \{\boxed{+}\ atom\}$$
$$atom = \boxed{(}\,expr\boxed{)}\ \big|\ \boxed{E}$$

admit each of the following as an *expr*

```
E               E - E              E + E
( E )           E - ( E - E )      E + E + E
( E + E )       ( E - E ) - E      E + E + E + E
```

A set of horizontal braces represents a component which may be omitted, or may be repeated any number of times in a vertical column, each instance having the same indentation. The production

$$sequence = \boxed{\text{SEQ}} \qquad \Big|\ \boxed{\text{SKIP}}$$
$$\underbrace{sequence}$$

admits each of

```
SEQ             SEQ                SEQ                SEQ
                SEQ                SKIP               SEQ
                                   SEQ               SKIP
                                                     SEQ
                                                     SEQ
```

as a *sequence*.

The notation is unambiguous except in the case of

$$process = declaration \; \boxed{:}$$
$$process$$

where the *declaration* can take up more than one line. In that case, I mean that a colon follows the last thing on the last line of the *declaration*. The awkwardness of that statement is reflected by a corresponding awkwardness in every *occam* parser that I have seen.

Processes

The unit of program structure is the process

$$process = action \,|\, construct \,|\, substitution \,|\, block$$

Processes may be one of a family of primitive *actions*, may be constructed from smaller processes, or may be invocations of named processes. Declarations may precede any process which is then the scope of these declarations.

The primitive processes may change the values of variables, communicate with other processes, or suspend execution.

$$action = \boxed{SKIP} \,|\, \boxed{STOP} \,|\, assignment \,|\, input \,|\, output \,|\, timer \,|\, delay$$

SKIP is the process that has no effect: it always executes to completion, and never does anything else. STOP is similar, in that it does nothing, but differs in that it never terminates.

Assignment

Assignment processes compute the values of expressions, and store them in variables.

$$assignment = variable \; \boxed{:=} \; expression \,|\, vectorvar \; \boxed{:=} \; vectorexpr$$

A simple assignment selects a *variable*, computes the value of the *expression*, and stores that value in that *variable*. Nothing else is changed.

A slice assignment copies values from its *vectorexpr* to the corresponding variables of its *vectorvar*. For a vector assignment to be valid, both vectors must be of the same size, both must be byte-vectors or both word-vectors, and they may not overlap.

Communications

Communication processes co-operate to implement distributed assignments by synchronizing two concurrent processes. The computation of the values is carried out in *output* processes, and the storing of values in *input* processes.

$$input \; = \quad channel \; \boxed{?} \; target \; \{\boxed{;} \; target\}$$

$$target \; = \quad variable \mid vectorvar \mid \boxed{\text{ANY}}$$

An *input* process selects a *channel*, selects its *variable* or vector of variables, and suspends execution until an *output* process is executing using the same channel. The notation

$$channel \; ? \; target \; ; \; targets$$

abbreviates

        SEQ
            channel ? target
            channel ? targets

No variable in any *target* may appear in the *channel*.

$$output \; = \quad channel \; \boxed{!} \; source \; \{\boxed{;} \; source\}$$

$$source \; = \quad expression \mid vectorexpr \mid \boxed{\text{ANY}}$$

An *output* process selects a *channel*, evaluates its *expression* or selects its vector of expressions, and suspends execution until an *input* process is executing using the same channel. The notation

$$channel \; ! \; source \; ; \; sources$$

abbreviates

        SEQ
            channel ! source
            channel ! sources

When an *input* and an *output* process are both executing using the same channel, the value of the *source* is stored in the *target* as though by the assignment

$$target \; := \; source$$

and both *input* and *output* terminate. Byte-vector outputs must correspond to byte-vector inputs, word-vector outputs to word-vector outputs, and the sizes of the both vectors must be the same. If the *target* is ANY, the assignment is not performed; if the *source* is ANY, an arbitrary value may be assigned.

Real-time processes

The *timer* process sets a selected *variable* to a value, notionally the present reading on a clock.

$$timer = \boxed{\text{TIME}} \ \boxed{?} \ variable$$

The clock reading changes with the passage of time, changing at regular intervals and counting up cyclically through the whole range representable numbers at a constant rate.

A *delay* suspends execution until the reading on the clock represents a time after a given one, to within the range of the clock.

$$delay = \boxed{\text{TIME}} \ \boxed{?} \ \boxed{\text{AFTER}} \ expression$$

It terminates with no other effect at some time after the reading on the clock has satisfied the relation *clock* AFTER *expression*.

Constructed processes

Compound processes execute either by executing their components in sequence or in parallel, or by selecting a component to be executed.

$$construct = sequence \, | \, conditional \, | \, parallel \, | \, alternative \, | \, repetition$$

Processes constructed by SEQ execute by executing all their components in sequence.

$$sequence = \boxed{\text{SEQ}} \underbrace{}_{process} \Big| \boxed{\text{SEQ}} \ replicator$$
$$process$$

A *sequence* starts with the execution of its first component process, each subsequent process starts if and when its predecessor has terminated, and the whole sequence terminates when and only when the last component has terminated.

A *sequence* is invalid if there is a channel which may be used only for input by one of its components, and only for output by another of its components.

Processes constructed by IF execute by executing one of their components, the selection of the component depending on the values of variables.

$$conditional = \boxed{\text{IF}} \underbrace{}_{choice} \Big| \boxed{\text{IF}} \ replicator$$
$$choice$$

$$choice \quad = \quad expression \, \Big| \, conditional$$
$$process$$

When a *conditional* executes it evaluates the *expressions* guarding its *choices* and those of its components. The expressions should evaluate to TRUE or to FALSE. A simple *choice* is ready if its condition is TRUE, and a *conditional* is ready if it has a ready component. A ready *conditional* executes by executing the first of its ready components, and a ready simple *choice* executes by executing its *process* part. An unready *conditional* executes exactly like STOP, and fails to terminate.

Processes constructed by PAR execute by the concurrent execution of all their components.

$$parallel = \boxed{PAR} \qquad \boxed{PAR}\ replicator$$
$$\underbrace{process} \qquad process$$

When a *parallel* construct executes, each of its component processes is executed. The whole construct terminates when and only when all of the components have terminated.

A *parallel* construct is invalid if any of its components may change the value of a variable which may be used in any other of its components. It is similarly invalid if there is a channel which may be used by two of the component processes, both using the channel for input, or both using it for output.

Processes constructed by ALT execute by executing one of their components, the selection of the component depending on the readiness of other processes to communicate.

$$alternative \quad = \quad [\boxed{PRI}]\ symmetricalt$$
$$symmetricalt = \boxed{ALT} \qquad \boxed{ALT}\ replicator$$
$$\underbrace{guarded} \qquad guarded$$

$$guarded \quad = \quad guard \quad | \quad symmetricalt$$
$$process \quad |$$

A simple *guarded* process is ready if its *guard* is ready, and a *symmetricalt* is ready if it has a ready *guarded* component. A ready *symmetricalt* executes by executing one of its ready components, and a ready simple *guarded* process executes by executing its *guard* and its *process* part in sequence. Executing an unready *symmetricalt* suspends execution until it should become ready. One of its components is then selected from amongst those that become ready simultaneously with the first to become ready.

If the whole *alternative* is preceded by PRI the first ready component is chosen whenever a choice is made, and each of its *symmetricalt* components behaves as though they too were preceded by PRI.

The readiness of a simple *guarded* process is determined by the readiness of its *guard.*

$$guard \ = \ \big[expression \ \boxed{\&}\big] \ atomic$$
$$atomic = \ input \big| \, delay \big| \, \boxed{SKIP}$$

The *expression* should evaluate to TRUE or to FALSE, and a *guard* is ready if and only if its *expression* is TRUE and its *atomic* action is ready. An omitted *expression* is treated as if it were the constant TRUE. A SKIP is always ready, a *delay* is ready when the clock reading has satisfied its condition, and an *input* is ready when the *output* corresponding to it has begun. Thus, an *atomic* action is ready when it can be executed to completion, or in the case of a multiple *input* when the first of its inputs can be executed to completion.

A *guard* executes by executing the *atomic* process part.

Regular arrays of processes are composed by replication from the constructors above.

$$replicator = \ name \ \boxed{=} \ \boxed{[} expression \ \boxed{FOR} \ expression \boxed{]} \big|$$

A *replicator* attached to a constructor replicates the single component of that construct, introducing in each copy a new binding for its *name.* The value of the second *expression*, which must be non-negative, gives the number of replications.

For each array constructor CONS,

$$\text{CONS } i = [b \text{ FOR } c]$$
$$component$$

is the same as an empty CONS construction if the value of c is zero. If the value of c is one, it is the same as a CONS construction with one component the same as *component* except that i is bound to the value of b. For larger positive c, it is equivalent to

```
CONS
    CONS i = [b FOR 1]
        component
    CONS i = [(b)+1  FOR (c)-1]
        component
```

The only form of unbounded loop is the sequential loop

$$repetition = \boxed{\text{WHILE}} \; expression$$
$$process$$

which executes exactly as though it were

```
IF
  expression
    SEQ
      process
      WHILE expression
        process
  NOT (expression)
    SKIP
```

Declarations

Declarations and definitions bind identifiers to constants, variables, channels and named processes.

$$block \qquad = \quad declaration \; \boxed{:}$$
$$process$$
$$declaration = \quad constdefs \mid vardecls \mid chandecls \mid procdecl$$

If a *declaration* precedes the *process*, then free occurrences in that *process* of the name which it introduces are bound by that *declaration*.
For each kind declaration for which it is legal,

```
DECL declaration, declarations :
process
```

abbreviates

```
DECL declaration :
DECL declarations :
process
```

A constant definition makes a new binding of a *name* to a constant value or vector of constant values.

$$constdefs = \quad \boxed{\text{CONST}} \; constdef \; \{\boxed{,} \; constdef\}$$
$$constdef \; = \quad name \; \boxed{=} \; expression \mid name \; \boxed{=} \; vectorexpr$$

In the scope of the definition, the *name* can be used as if it were a
constant or vector of constants as appropriate. Its value is that of
the *expression* or *vectorexpr*.

An expression is a compilation constant if every name in it is
bound by a constant definition. All expressions appearing in constant
definitions must be compilation constants.

A variable declaration introduces a new variable or vector of
variables, and binds a *name* to that variable or vector.

$$vardecls = \boxed{\text{VAR}} \; vardecl \; \{ \boxed{,} \; vardecl \}$$

$$vardecl \; = \; name \,\big|\, name \boxed{[} \, \boxed{\text{BYTE}} \, expression \boxed{]}$$

A declaration consisting of a *name* alone introduces a simple variable.

If the *name* is followed by an *expression* in brackets, a vector of
new variables is introduced. The value of the *expression*, which must
be positive, is the number of variables in the vector. The word BYTE
inside the left bracket indicates a vector of byte variables.

$$variable \; = \; name \,\big|\, vectorvar \; selector$$

$$vectorvar = \; name \,\big|\, vectorvar \; slicer$$

If a value is to be stored in a byte variable selected from a vector,
the value is truncated to its least significant eight bits before being
stored.

A channel declaration introduces a new channel or vector of
channels, and binds a name to the new channel or vector.

$$chandecls = \boxed{\text{CHAN}} \; chandecl \; \{ \boxed{,} \; chandecl \}$$

$$chandecl \; = \; name \,\big|\, name \; \boxed{[} expression \boxed{]}$$

A declaration consisting of a *name* alone introduces a new channel.
If the *name* is followed by an *expression* in brackets, a vector of new
channels is introduced. The value of the *expression*, which must be
positive, is the number of channels in the vector.

A *channel* is denoted by a *name* bound to a channel, or by selecting one from a vector of channels.

$$channel = \; name \,\big|\, name \; \boxed{[} expression \boxed{]}$$

A channel selection is valid if the *name* is bound to a vector of channels, and the value of the *expression* in brackets is non-negative and
less than the number of channels in that vector. The channels in
a vector are indexed consecutively from zero for the first, and the
channel selected is that indexed by the value of the *expression*.

Named processes

A name may be bound to a process

$$procdecl \quad = \quad \boxed{\text{PROC}} \; name \; \big[formals\big] \; \boxed{=}$$
$$process$$

$$substitution = \quad name \; \big[actuals\big]$$

so that in the scope of

$$\text{PROC } name =$$
$$process$$

the *name* may appear with the same meaning as the *process*. Names free in the text of the *process* and not bound by parameters of the process declaration are bound in the environment of the declaration.

The *process* is the scope of bindings of those names which appear as formal parameters in the declaration

$$formals = \quad \boxed{(} \; formal \; \big\{\boxed{,} \; formal\big\} \; \boxed{)}$$

$$formal \; = \quad constformals \, \big| \, varformals \, \big| \, chanformals$$

to the meanings of actual parameters that appear at the point of each substitution

$$actuals = \quad \boxed{(} \; actual \; \big\{\boxed{,} \; actual\big\} \; \boxed{)}$$

$$actual \; = \quad constactual \, \big| \, varactual \, \big| \, chanactual$$

The number and kinds of formal and actual parameters must correspond. In each case,

$$\text{KEY } formal, \; formals$$

abbreviates

$$\text{KEY } formal, \; \text{KEY } formals$$

Constant parameters bind names to the values or vectors of values.

$$constformals = \quad \boxed{\text{VALUE}} \; constformal \; \big\{\boxed{,} \; constformal\big\}$$

$$constformal \; = \quad name \, \big| \, name \; \boxed{[}\,\boxed{]}$$

$$constactual \; = \quad expression \, \big| \, vectorexpr$$

A *name* appearing alone as a *constformal* must be bound to the value of an *expression*, and a *name* followed by a pair of brackets must be bound to a vector of values.

Variable parameters bind names to variables or vectors of variables.

$$varformals = \boxed{\text{VAR}}\ varformal\ \{\boxed{,}\ varformal\}$$

$$varformal = name\ |\ name\ \boxed{[}\boxed{]}$$

$$varactual = variable\ |\ vectorvar$$

A *name* appearing alone as a *varformal* must be bound to a simple variable, which must not be a byte variable selected from a vector. A *name* followed by a pair of brackets must be bound to a vector of variables, which must not be a byte slice of a vector.

Channel parameters bind names to channels or vectors of channels.

$$chanformals = \boxed{\text{CHAN}}\ chanformal\ \{\boxed{,}\ chanformal\}$$

$$chanformal = name\ |\ name\ \boxed{[}\boxed{]}$$

$$chanactual = channel\ |\ name$$

A *name* appearing alone as a *chanformal* must be bound to a simple channel, and a *name* followed by a pair of brackets must be bound to a vector of channels.

Expressions

The simplest expressions are literal constants

$$literal = numeral\ |\ \boxed{\text{TRUE}}\ |\ \boxed{\text{FALSE}}$$

The value of a *numeral* was described informally above. The value of TRUE is a word in which every bit is one, and the value of FALSE is a word in which every bit is zero.

$$rand = name\ |\ literal\ |\ selection\ |\ \boxed{(}\ expression\ \boxed{)}$$

A *name* may appear as an operand if it is bound to a constant, in which case its value is that constant; if it is bound to a value by a *replicator*, or by a VALUE parameter, then that value; if it is bound to a variable in which a value has been stored, then the value most recently stored in that variable. The value of a *selection* is the selected component of the vector of values. Any *expression* in brackets can appear as an operand, having the value of the *expression*.

$$expression = \quad rand\,[rator\,rand]\,|\,rand\,\{assoc\,rand\}\,|\,signed$$

$$signed \quad = \quad signednumeral\,|\,monop\,rand$$

Expressions are fully bracketed combinations of operands and operators

$$rator \quad = \quad arithmetic\,|\,comparison\,|\,logical\,|\,boolean\,|\,shift$$

$$monop = \quad \boxed{-}\,|\,\boxed{\text{NOT}}$$

except that the brackets may be omitted from sequences of operands joined by the same associative operator

$$assoc = \boxed{+}\,|\,\boxed{*}\,|\,logical\,|\,boolean$$

The *arithmetic* operators treat their operands as signed twos-complement representations of integers.

$$arithmetic = \boxed{+}\,|\,\boxed{-}\,|\,\boxed{*}\,|\,\boxed{/}\,|\,\boxed{\backslash}$$

The value of **a + b** is the sum of (the values of) *a* and *b*

        a - b   the difference of *a* and *b*

        a * b   the product of *a* and *b*

        a / b   the result of dividing *a* by *b*

        a \ b   the remainder on dividing *a* by *b*

provided that the value has a twos-complement representation as a word-sized bit pattern. The result of division is an integer and is rounded towards zero in case it cannot be exact, so that provided that *b* is not zero, nor is *a* the most negative representable integer and *b* minus one,

$$a = ((b * (a/b)) + (a\backslash b))$$

and the sign of the remainder is that of *a*.

The monadic subtraction operator negates its argument, so that

$$(- a) = (0 - a)$$

The value of an expression in a comparison operator is TRUE or FALSE according to a test on the values of the operands.

$$comparison = \boxed{<}\;\boxed{<=}\;\boxed{=}\;\boxed{>}\;\boxed{>=}\;\boxed{<>}\;\boxed{\text{AFTER}}$$

The value of **a < b** is TRUE if a is less than b

a <= b	if a is not more than b
a = b	if a is the same as b
a >= b	if a is not less than b
a > b	if a is more than b
a <> b	if a is not the same as b

and is FALSE otherwise.

Let h be the smallest positive integer that is too large to have a twos-complement representation as a word sized bit-pattern. The value of **a AFTER b** is TRUE   if $a < b$ and $(a - b) < h$
or $a > b$ and $(b - a) > h$
and is FALSE otherwise.

Each bit in the value of an expression in a logical operator

$$logical = \boxed{/\backslash}\;\boxed{\backslash/}\;\boxed{><}$$

is determined by applying the operator to corresponding bits of the operands, according to the rules

$$0 \;/\backslash\; b = 0$$
$$1 \;/\backslash\; b = b$$
$$0 \;\backslash/\; b = b$$
$$1 \;\backslash/\; b = 1$$
$$0 \;><\; b = b$$
$$b \;><\; 0 = b$$
$$1 \;><\; 1 = 0$$

where b is either 0 or 1. The monadic operator NOT complements each bit of its argument.

Expressions in the Boolean operators

$$boolean = \boxed{\text{AND}}\;\boxed{\text{OR}}$$

are evaluated consistently with the rules

TRUE AND b	= b
FALSE AND b	= FALSE
TRUE OR b	= TRUE
FALSE OR b	= b

The right operand may be an expression with no defined meaning (such as a division by zero) in case the value of the whole expression does not depend on it.

The value of an expression in a *shift* operator is the same bit pattern as the left operand, displaced by a number of bits given by the right operand.

$$shift = \boxed{<<} \,\big|\, \boxed{>>}$$

The value of a << b is   *a* displaced left by *b* bit positions

  a >> b   *a* displaced right by *b* bit positions

provided that the value of *b* is not negative. Bits in a pattern shifted left are moved to more significant positions, and in a pattern shifted right are moved to less significant positions. Vacant bit positions are filled by zero bits, and bits shifted past the boundary of the word are discarded.

Vector expressions

A vector expression has a value which is a finite sequence of values.

$$vectorexpr = name \,\big|\, string \,\big|\, table \,\big|\, slice$$

A *name* has a vector value if it is bound by a constant definition to a constant vector, in which case the value is that constant vector; by a **VALUE** vector formal parameter, in which case the value is that of the corresponding actual parameter; by a variable vector declaration or by a **VAR** vector formal, in which case the value is the vector of values most recently stored in the variables.

The value of a *string* is the constant byte vector described above. The value of a *table* expression

$$table = \boxed{\text{TABLE}} \;\; \boxed{[} \,\boxed{\text{BYTE}}\big|\, expression \,\big\{\,\boxed{,} \; expression\big\}\,\boxed{]}$$

is also a constant vector, with as many components as there are component expressions, the value of each component being the value of the corresponding expression. Each expression must be a compilation constant. If the word **BYTE** appears inside the left bracket, the value of the *table* is a vector of byte constants, the value of each component of which is the least significant eight bits of the value of the corresponding *expression*.

A single value can be selected from a vector by subscription

$$selection = vectorexpr \; selector$$

$$selector = \boxed{[} \,\boxed{\text{BYTE}}\big|\, expression \,\boxed{]}$$

The value of the selecting *expression* must be non-negative and less than the number of components in the vector. The components of a vector are indexed consecutively from zero at the first component, and the value of a *selection* is that component of the value of the *vector* indexed by the value of the *expression*.

A *selector* selects a word from a word vector, unless BYTE appears inside the left bracket in which case it selects a byte from a byte vector.

A *slice* of a vector is also a vector.

$$slice \ = \ vectorexpr \ slicer$$

$$slicer = \ \boxed{[}\,\boxed{[\,\boxed{\text{BYTE}}\,]}\,expression\ \boxed{\text{FOR}}\ expression\boxed{]}$$

A word vector sliced by a word slicer is a word vector, and a byte slice, with BYTE inside the left bracket, of a byte vector is a byte vector. The first component of the value of the *slice* is that indexed by the value of the first *expression* of the *slicer*. The number of components in the value of a *slice* is the value of the second *expression* in the *slicer*, which must be positive. The correspondence is such that

```
p[q FOR r][s]         = p[(q) + (s)]
p[BYTE q FOR r][BYTE s] = p[BYTE (q) + (s)]
```

For a *slice* to be valid, each valid selection from it must be a valid selection from the vector, according to these rules.

Implementation dependencies

An implementation may require some expressions to have values which are readily determinable during compilation. Any name which occurs in such a compilation constant must be bound by a constant definition. The expressions in constant definitions and tables must always be constants. Conventional implementations will require the sizes of declared vectors of variables and channels, and the replication counts of PAR replicators also to be constants.

The language described in the *occam Programming Manual* allows of byte selection and slicing of word vectors and vice versa. The meanings of programs which use these depend on an implementation parameter N which is the number of bytes in a word. The values of word and byte vectors are identified in such a way that

```
p[BYTE q] = (p[(q)/N] >> ((q)\N)) /\#FF
```

and consistently for slices.

Configuration directives

Although an *occam* program may simply be a process, the *Programming Manual* defines constructions for configuring stand-alone programs.

$$program \ = \ system \left| \begin{array}{l} allocation \\ singleton \end{array} \right| \begin{array}{l} global \\ program \end{array}$$

A *program* may be a *system* of processes to be run on different processors, or it may be a *singleton* to be run on a single processor. (An *allocation* includes the information necessary for a compiler to fit the *singleton* to its processor. Although the *Programming Manual* describes this, it is of no interest in this book so left undescribed.)

Declarations which precede a distributed program must themselves be distributable

$$globals \ = \ constdefs \left| \, chandecls \, \right| procdecl$$

so may not declare any variables. Their meaning is exactly the same as it would have been in an ordinary *block*.

A *system* of distributed processes is divided between processors by indicating the distribution of the outermost parallel constructs.

$$system \ = \ \boxed{\text{PLACED}} \ \boxed{\text{PAR}} \left| \, \boxed{\text{PLACED}} \ \boxed{\text{PAR}} \, replicator \right.$$
$$\underbrace{program} \quad \left| \quad program \right.$$

A *system* executes by the concurrent execution of its component programs. The annotation PLACED does not alter the execution of a *parallel* except to indicate that each component is to be executed by a different (set of) processors.

A *singleton* is to be executed by a single processor.

$$singleton \ = \ process \left| \, \boxed{\text{PRI}} \ \boxed{\text{PAR}} \, \right| \begin{array}{l} declaration \ \boxed{:} \\ singleton \end{array}$$
$$\underbrace{process}$$

A *singleton* may either be a *process* to be executed by its processor, or an asymmetric *parallel*.

An asymmetric *parallel* executes by the concurrent execution of its component processes, in the same way as the corresponding symmetric construct, except that it is guaranteed that no component executes unless all syntactically preceding components are unable to proceed, either because they are waiting for communication or because they have terminated. An implementation may impose a small limit on the number of components in an asymmetric *parallel*.

A *declaration* preceding an asymmetric *parallel* has exactly the same meaning as if the *parallel* were symmetric.

Index of definitions

Codes of the Programs

In the following pages are the programs referred to in the corresponding-ly named chapters earlier in the book. They are transcribed as faithfully as circumstances permitted from originals composed and executed using an *occam* programming system.

In the transcription, the structure of the text has been removed, leaving only the sequence of lines which you see here. It is harder to read 'flat', un-folded *occam* on paper than it is to read a structured text using an editor that allows exploration of that structure. In recognition of this difficulty there is, on the title page of each section, a summary of the gross structure of the code which follows in that section.

Input and output routines

```
PROC write.string(CHAN output, VALUE string[])
  -- Write the characters of the string[] to the output

PROC write.signed(CHAN output, VALUE n, field.width)
  -- Write a signed decimal representation of n to the output,
  -- right justified to occupy field.width character spaces

PROC read.signed(CHAN input, VAR n, ok)
  -- Read an (optionally signed) decimal numeral from the input
  -- returning the corresponding value in n, and TRUE or FALSE
  -- in ok according as the conversion worked or not

PROC read.line(CHAN keyboard, screen, VAR s[])
  -- Construct a string in s[] from the printable characters
  -- read from keyboard and echoed to screen. The string
  -- finishes at a carriage return.
```

144

```
PROC write.string(CHAN output, VALUE string[]) =
  -- Write the characters of the string[] to the output
  SEQ character.number = [1 FOR string[BYTE 0]]
    output ! string[BYTE character.number]        :



PROC write.signed(CHAN output, VALUE n, field.width) =
  -- Write a signed decimal representation of n to the output,
  -- right justified to occupy field.width character spaces
  VAR tens, width :            -- tens will be a signed power of ten
  SEQ
    IF
      n >= 0
        SEQ
          tens  := -1
          width := 1        -- count a minimum of one digit
      n < 0
        SEQ
          tens  := 1
          width := 2        -- count a sign and a minimum of one digit

    WHILE (n / tens) <= (-10)   -- set tens so that  0<(-(n/tens))<=10
      SEQ                       -- or, if n = 0 then tens = -1
        tens  := 10 * tens
        width := width + 1

    WHILE width < field.width   -- pad with spaces to field.width
      SEQ
        output ! '*s'
        width := width + 1

    IF                          -- output a sign for negative n
      n >= 0
        SKIP
      n < 0
        output ! '-'

    WHILE tens <> 0 -- output the digits of n, most significant first
      SEQ
        output ! '0' - ((n / tens) \ 10)
        tens := tens / 10                   :
```

```
PROC read.signed(CHAN input, VAR n, ok) =
  -- Read an (optionally signed) decimal numeral from the input
  -- returning the corresponding value in n, and TRUE or FALSE in
  -- ok according as the conversion worked or not

  DEF min = NOT ((NOT 0) >> 1), max = (NOT 0) >> 1 :
  DEF otherwise = TRUE :

  VAR ch, sign :
  SEQ

    input ? ch
    WHILE ch = '*s'                -- skip leading spaces
      input ? ch

    IF
      (ch = '+') OR (ch = '-')     -- read a possible sign
        SEQ
          sign := ch
          input ? ch
      (ch <> '+') AND (ch <> '-')
        sign := '+'

    WHILE ch = '*s'                -- skip any spaces after the sign
      input ? ch

    n := 0
    ok := ('0' <= ch) AND (ch <= '9')  -- check for digits

    WHILE ('0' <= ch) AND (ch <= '9')  -- and read a sequence of them
      SEQ
        IF
          (sign = '+') AND (n <= ((max - (ch - '0')) / 10))
            n := (10 * n) + (ch - '0')
          (sign = '-') AND (((min + (ch - '0')) / 10) <= n)
            n := (10 * n) - (ch - '0')
          otherwise
            ok := FALSE                -- number out of representable range
        input ? ch                   :
```

```
PROC read.line(CHAN keyboard, screen, VAR s[]) =
  -- Construct a string in s[] from the printable characters
  -- read from keyboard and echoed to screen. The string
  -- finishes at a carriage return.

  DEF control    = NOT ((NOT 0) << 5),
      otherwise  = TRUE,
      backspace  = control /\ 'H',
      bell       = control /\ 'G',
      cancel     = control /\ 'U',
      delete     = NOT ((NOT 0) << 7),
      max.length = NOT ((NOT 0) << 8) :

  SEQ
    s[BYTE 0] := 0         -- byte zero contains the length of the string
    WHILE s[BYTE s[BYTE 0]] <> '*C'
    VAR ch :
    keyboard ? ch
    IF
      ('*S' <= ch) AND (ch < delete) AND
                              (s[BYTE 0] < (max.length - 1))
        SEQ                              -- 'printable' characters are
          screen ! ch                    --      echoed
          s[BYTE 0] := s[BYTE 0] + 1
          s[BYTE s[BYTE 0]] := ch        --      and added to the string
      ch = '*C'
        SEQ                              -- carriage return
          s[BYTE 0] := s[BYTE 0] + 1     --      is added to the string
          s[BYTE s[BYTE 0]] := ch        --      and terminates the loop
      (ch = backspace) AND (s[BYTE 0] > 0)
        SEQ                              -- backspace
          screen ! backspace ; '*S'      --   overwrites the last
          screen ! backspace             --   character echoed
          s[BYTE 0] := s[BYTE 0] - 1     --   and removes it from the
                                         --   string
      ch = cancel
        WHILE s[BYTE 0] > 0              -- cancel
          SEQ                            --   backspaces over the
                                         --   whole of the line
            screen ! backspace ; '*S' ; backspace
            s[BYTE 0] := s[BYTE 0] - 1
      otherwise                          -- anything else is an error
        screen ! bell                          :
```

Terminal interrupt management

```
PROC keyboard.handler(CHAN request, sink, error)
  -- Characters typed at the keyboard can be read from sink.
  -- A signal is required on request before each item is read.

PROC echo.handler(CHAN request, reply, echo, inward)
  -- Read characters from a buffer by request/reply, passing
  -- them on to the inward channel with a copy to echo

PROC output.multiplexer(CHAN from[],VALUE width,CHAN outgoing)
  -- Copy characters from each of from[0 FOR width] to outgoing
  -- switching between inputs on receipt of a release value

PROC screen.handler(CHAN outgoing, error)
  -- Forwards characters from channel outgoing to the screen
  -- and rings a bell in case of a signal on the error channel

PROC user(CHAN terminal.keyboard, terminal.screen)
  -- Template for the user's program

PRI PAR

  PAR    -- High priority process
    --

  PAR    -- Low priority process
    --
```

```
DEF type.ahead = ...,  control = NOT ((NOT 0) << 5),  release = -1 :


PROC keyboard.handler(CHAN request, sink, error) =
  -- Characters typed at the keyboard can be read from sink.
  -- A signal is required on request before each item is read.
  -- If more than type.ahead are typed-ahead, an error is signalled.
  CHAN keystroke.in AT ... :
  VAR reader, writer, count :
  SEQ
    reader  := 0          -- index of next item to be read from buffer
    writer  := 0          -- index of next free location in buffer
    count   := type.ahead -- number of spare locations in buffer
    VAR datum[type.ahead] :
    WHILE TRUE
      ALT
        count = 0 &                      -- if no room
               keystroke.in ? ANY    -- but something is typed
          error ! ANY                 --        then signal an error
        count > 0 &                      -- if there is room and
               keystroke.in ? datum[writer]  -- something is typed
          SEQ                                --        then store it
            writer  := (writer + 1) \ type.ahead
            count   := count - 1
        count < type.ahead &             -- if something in the buffer
               request ? ANY          -- and something is requested
          SEQ                            --    then read from the buffer
            sink ! datum[reader]
            reader  := (reader + 1) \ type.ahead
            count   := count + 1                  :


PROC echo.handler(CHAN request, reply, echo, inward) =
  -- Read characters from a buffer by request/reply, passing
  -- them on to the inward channel with a copy to echo
  DEF enter = control /\ 'M' :
  WHILE TRUE
    VAR ch :
    SEQ
      request ! ANY
      reply ? ch
      inward ! ch                     -- transmit character to user
      IF
        ('*s' <= ch)  AND  (ch <= ' ') -- visible input
          echo ! ch                    --   sent to terminal screen
        ch = enter                     -- at the end of a line
          echo ! release               --   release the screen
        TRUE
          SKIP                   :
```

```
PROC output.multiplexer(CHAN from[], VALUE width, CHAN outgoing) =
  -- Copy characters from each of from[O FOR width] to outgoing
  -- switching between inputs on receipt of a release value
  WHILE TRUE
  VAR ch :
  ALT selected.process = [O FOR width]
    from[selected.process] ? ch  -- take a message from any of from[]
      WHILE ch <> release        -- and copy it to completion
      SEQ
          outgoing ! ch
          from[selected.process] ? ch                    :



PROC screen.handler(CHAN outgoing, error) =
  -- Forwards characters from channel outgoing to the screen
  -- and rings a bell in case of a signal on the error channel
  DEF bell.character = control /\ 'G' :
  CHAN screen.out AT ... :
  WHILE TRUE
    VAR ch :
    PRI ALT
      error ? ANY               -- signal errors by ringing the bell
        screen.out ! bell.character
      outgoing ? ch             -- and send on outgoing characters
        screen.out ! ch                 :




PROC user(CHAN terminal.keyboard, terminal.screen) =
  ... Template for the user's program



DEF  from.echo.handler = 0. from.user = 1, number.of.outputs = 2 :
CHAN outgoing, from.keyboard, to.screen[number.of.outputs] :

PRI PAR

  CHAN request, reply, error :          -- High priority process
  PAR
    keyboard.handler(request, reply, error)
    echo.handler(request, reply,
                      to.screen[from.echo.handler], from.keyboard)
    screen.handler(outgoing, error)

  PAR                                   -- Low priority process
    output.multiplexer(to.screen, number.of.outputs, outgoing)
    user(from.keyboard, to.screen[from.user])
```

Parallel matrix multiplier

```
PROC produce.xj(VALUE j, CHAN south)
  -- north row: source of x values
PROC consume.yi(VALUE i, CHAN east)
  -- west column: sink for y values
PROC offset(VALUE ki, CHAN west)
  -- east column: source of k offsets
PROC multiplier(VALUE aij, CHAN north, south, west, east)
  -- middle: responsible for a values
PROC sink(CHAN north)
  -- south row: sink for unused outputs
SEQ
  -- initialize a and k
  PAR
    PAR j = [0 FOR n]
      produce.xj(j, ...)
    PAR i = [0 FOR n]
      offset(k[i], ...)
    PAR i = [0 FOR n]
      PAR j = [0 FOR n]
        multiplier( ... )
    PAR j = [0 FOR n]
      sink(...)
    PAR i = [0 FOR n]
      consume.yi(i, ...)
```

```
PROC produce.xj(VALUE j, CHAN south) = -- north row: source x values
  WHILE TRUE
    south ! ANY                       :



PROC consume.yi(VALUE i, CHAN east) =  -- west column: sink y values
  WHILE TRUE
    east ? ANY                        :



PROC offset(VALUE ki, CHAN west) =        -- east column: source k offsets
  WHILE TRUE
    west ! ki                         :



PROC multiplier(VALUE aij, CHAN north, south, west, east) =
  VAR xj, aij.times.xj, yi :              -- responsible for a values
  SEQ
    north ? xj
    WHILE TRUE
      SEQ
        PAR
          south ! xj
          aij.times.xj := aij * xj
          east ? yi
        PAR
          west ! yi + aij.times.xj
          north ? xj                  :



PROC sink(CHAN north) =                 -- south row
  WHILE TRUE                           --    sink for unused outputs
    north ? ANY          :
```

```
DEF n = 3 :
VAR a[n * n],  k[n] :
SEQ
  -- initialize a and k

  CHAN north.south[n * (n + 1)],  east.west[n * (n + 1)] :
  PAR
    PAR j = [O FOR n]
      produce.xj(j, north.south[j])

    PAR i = [O FOR n]
      offset(k[i], east.west[(n * n) + i])
    PAR i = [O FOR n]
      PAR j = [O FOR n]
        multiplier( a[(n * i) + j],
                    north.south [(n * i) + j],
                    north.south [(n * (i + 1)) + j],
                    east.west   [i + (n * j)],
                    east.west   [i + (n * (j + 1))] )
    PAR j = [O FOR n]
      sink(north.south[(n * n) + j])

    PAR i = [O FOR n]
      consume.yi(i, east.west[i])
```

Parallel sorter

```
PROC fork(CHAN up,down, left.down,left.up, right.down,right.up)
  PROC fork.distribute(CHAN up, left.up, right.up)
  PROC fork.gather(CHAN down, left.down, right.down)
PROC leaf(CHAN up, down, probe)

PROC monitor(CHAN up.a, down.a, up.b, down.b, probe)
PROC multiplex(CHAN probe[], all.probes)
PROC independent(CHAN source, sink)
  PROC make.cartesian(VALUE index, VAR x, y)
PROC dependent(CHAN source, terminal)
  PROC clear.screen(CHAN terminal)
  PROC goto.xy(CHAN terminal, VALUE x, y)
PROC display(CHAN source, sink)
PROC driver(CHAN up, down)
  PROC shift(VAR state)

PAR
  driver(up.a[root], down.b[root])
  PAR i = [first.fork FOR number.of.forks]
    fork( ... )
  PAR i = [first.leaf FOR number.of.leaves]
    leaf( ... )
  PAR i = [root FOR number.of.channels]
    monitor( ... )
  multiplex(probe, all.probes)
  display(all.probes, terminal.screen)
```

```
PROC fork(CHAN up, down, left.down, left.up, right.down, right.up) =

  PROC fork.distribute(CHAN up, left.up, right.up) =
    -- share out a sequence of numbers as two sequences
    -- to the left, to the right
    DEF leftward = 0, rightward = NOT leftward :
    VAR more, inclination :
    SEQ
      inclination := leftward
      up ? more
      WHILE more
        VAR number :
        SEQ
          up ? number
          IF
            inclination = leftward
              left.up ! TRUE; number
            inclination = rightward
              right.up ! TRUE; number
          up ? more
          inclination := NOT inclination
      PAR
        left.up ! FALSE
        right.up ! FALSE                          :

  PROC fork.gather(CHAN down, left.down, right.down) =
    -- merge two ascending sequences, from left and right
    -- into one ascending sequence
    VAR left.more, left.minimum, right.more, right.minimum :
    SEQ
      PAR
        left.down ? left.more; left.minimum
        right.down ? right.more; right.minimum
      WHILE left.more OR right.more
        IF
          left.more AND
                ((NOT right.more) OR (left.minimum <= right.minimum))
            SEQ
              down ! TRUE; left.minimum
              left.down ? left.more; left.minimum
          right.more AND
                ((NOT left.more) OR (left.minimum >= right.minimum))
            SEQ
              down ! TRUE; right.minimum
              right.down ? right.more; right.minimum
      down ! FALSE; ANY                           :

  -- PROC fork() -- actions for a medial node in the sorting tree
  SEQ
    fork.distribute(up, left.up, right.up)
    fork.gather(down, left.down, right.down)  :
```

```
DEF display.number = 1, display.empty = 2, display.stop = 3 :


PROC leaf(CHAN up, down, probe) =
  -- actions for a terminal node in the sorting tree
  VAR number :
  SEQ
    up ? ANY; number                -- expect a sequence of one number
    probe ! display.number; number  -- pass to the monitoring code
    up ? ANY
    down ! TRUE; number             -- return it as a sequence
    probe ! display.empty           -- indicating its departure
    down ! FALSE; ANY
    probe ! display.stop            :


PROC monitor(CHAN up.a, down.a, up.b, down.b, probe) =
  -- in-channel monitoring code, in the form of a buffer
  SEQ
    VAR more :
    SEQ                -- first watch an upward-bound sequence of values
      up.a ? more
      WHILE more
        VAR number :
        SEQ
          up.a ? number
          probe ! display.number; number
          up.b ! more; number
          probe ! display.empty
          up.a ? more
      up.b ! more
    VAR more, number :
    SEQ                -- then watch a downward-bound sequence
      down.a ? more; number
      WHILE more
        SEQ
          probe ! display.number; number
          down.b ! more; number
          probe ! display.empty
          down.a ? more; number
      down.b ! more; number
      probe ! display.stop                      :
```

```
DEF depth.of.tree = 4 :

DEF number.of.leaves     = 1 << depth.of.tree ,
    number.of.forks      = number.of.leaves - 1 ,
    number.of.processes = number.of.forks + number.of.leaves ,
    number.of.channels  = number.of.processes ,
    number.of.probes    = number.of.channels + number.of.leaves :


PROC multiplex(CHAN probe[], all.probes) =
  -- gather all probe signals onto a single channel
  VAR more, more.from[number.of.probes] :
  SEQ
    more := number.of.probes
    SEQ i = [0 FOR number.of.probes]
      more.from[i] := TRUE
    WHILE more > 0            -- while not all probes are dead
      VAR instruction :
      ALT i = [0 FOR number.of.probes]
        more.from[i] & probe[i] ? instruction
                                 -- take a probe instruction
          IF
            instruction = display.number    -- if this is a number
              VAR number :
              SEQ
                probe[i] ? number            -- copy the number
                all.probes ! instruction; i; number
                                 -- tagging it with the probe number

            instruction = display.empty    -- if this is a blank
              all.probes ! instruction; i
                                 -- tag it with the probe number

            instruction = display.stop     -- if the probe is dead
              SEQ
                more.from[i] := FALSE        -- then expect no more
                more := more - 1             -- and decrease the count
                                 --   of working ones
    all.probes ! display.stop      :
```

```
DEF field.width = 3 :

PROC independent(CHAN source, sink) =


  PROC make.cartesian(VALUE index, VAR x, y) =
    -- turn a probe index into Cartesian co-ordinates
    -- in a terminal-independent space
    IF
      IF line = [1 FOR depth.of.tree + 1]
        index < ((1 << line) - 1)           -- then probe is from a
          VAR c :                           --   channel at this depth
          SEQ
            c  := index - ((1 << (line - 1)) - 1)
            x := ((2 * c) + 1) * (number.of.leaves >> (line - 1))
            y := line
      index >= number.of.channels           -- then probe is from a leaf
        SEQ
          x := (2 * (index - number.of.channels)) + 1
          y := depth.of.tree + 2                          :


  VAR instruction :
  SEQ
    source ? instruction
    WHILE instruction <> display.stop
      SEQ                          -- turn every probe signal into ...
        sink ! TRUE                --      ... a TRUE value
        VAR index, x, y :
        SEQ
          source ? index
          make.cartesian(index, x, y)
          sink ! x; y              --      ... a co-ordinate-pair
        IF                         --      and field.width characters:
          instruction = display.number
            VAR number :
            SEQ
              source ? number
              write.signed(sink, number, field.width) -- a numeral
          instruction = display.empty
            SEQ i = [0 FOR field.width]                 -- or blanks
              sink ! '*s'
        source ? instruction
    sink ! FALSE                            :
```

```
DEF virtual.height = depth.of.tree + 1,
    virtual.width  = (2 * number.of.leaves) - 1 :


PROC dependent(CHAN source, terminal) =
  -- terminal dependent code for driving a VT52

  DEF screen.height = 24, screen.width = 80 :

  DEF control = NOT ((NOT 0) << 5), escape = control /\ '[' :

  PROC clear.screen(CHAN terminal) =
    -- clear screen sequence for a VT52
    terminal ! escape ; 'H' ; escape ; 'J'              :

  PROC goto.xy(CHAN terminal, VALUE x, y) =
    -- lefthanded co-ordinates, origin 0, 0 at top left
    terminal ! escape ; 'Y' ; '*s' + y ; '*s' + x    :

  VAR more :
  SEQ
    clear.screen(terminal)
    source ? more
    WHILE more
      SEQ
        VAR x, y :
        SEQ
          source ? x; y
          goto.xy(terminal, (x - 1) * (screen.width / virtual.width),
                (virtual.height - y) * (screen.height / virtual.height))
        SEQ i = [1 FOR field.width]
          VAR ch :
          SEQ
            source ? ch
            terminal ! ch
        source ? more
    goto.xy(terminal, 0, screen.height - 1)              :


PROC display(CHAN source, sink) =
  CHAN internal :
  PAR
    independent(source, internal)
    dependent(internal, sink)      :
```

```
PROC driver(CHAN up, down) =

  DEF mask = NOT ((NOT 0) << 9) :

  PROC shift(VAR state) =
    SEQ i = [1 FOR 9]
      state := ((state << 1) /\ mask) \/
                                 (((state >> 4) >< (state >> 8)) /\ 1)  :

  SEQ
    VAR event, number :                   -- first fill the tree
    SEQ
      TIME ? event
      number :=  (event /\ mask) \/ 1 -- initialize the random number
      SEQ i = [0 FOR number.of.leaves]
        SEQ
          event := event + second
          shift(number)                   -- pick a new number
          up ! TRUE; number               -- send it into the tree
          TIME ? AFTER event              -- and wait for a second
      up ! FALSE
    VAR event :                           -- then empty the tree
    SEQ
      TIME ? event
      SEQ i = [0 FOR number.of.leaves]
        SEQ
          event := event + second
          down ? ANY; ANY                 -- take a number from the tree
          TIME ? AFTER event              -- once a second
      down ? ANY; ANY                :
```

```
DEF root = 0 ,
   first.fork = root ,
   first.leaf = first.fork + number.of.forks :

CHAN  up.a[number.of.channels], down.a[number.of.channels],
      up.b[number.of.channels], down.b[number.of.channels],
      probe[number.of.probes], all.probes   :

PAR
  driver(up.a[root], down.b[root])

  PAR i = [first.fork FOR number.of.forks]
    fork(up.b[i], down.a[i],
         down.b[(2*i)+1], up.a[(2*i)+1],
         down.b[(2*i)+2], up.a[(2*i)+2])

  PAR i = [first.leaf FOR number.of.leaves]
    leaf(up.b[i], down.a[i],
         probe[number.of.channels + (i - first.leaf)])

  PAR i = [root FOR number.of.channels]
    monitor(up.a[i], down.a[i], up.b[i], down.b[i], probe[i])

  multiplex(probe, all.probes)

  display(all.probes, terminal.screen)
```

Conway's game of Life

```
PROC calculate.next.state(CHAN link[],
                          VALUE in[], state, VAR next.state)
PROC broadcast.present.state(CHAN link[], VALUE out[], state)
PROC cell(CHAN link[], VALUE in[], out[], CHAN control, sense)
PROC initialize(VALUE x, y, VAR in[], out[])

PROC move.cursor(CHAN screen, VALUE x, y)
PROC clear.screen(CHAN screen)

PROC initialize.display(CHAN screen)
PROC clean.up.display(CHAN screen)
PROC display.state(CHAN screen, VALUE x, y, state)

PROC generation(CHAN screen, control[], sense[], VAR active)

PROC edit(CHAN keyboard, screen, control[])

PROC display.activity(CHAN screen, VALUE activity)
PROC new.activity(VAR activity, VALUE ch)
PROC controller(CHAN keyboard, screen, control[], sense[])

PAR
  controller( ... )                -- control process
  PAR x = [0 FOR array.width]      -- board
    PAR y = [0 FOR array.height]
      SEQ
        initialize( ... )
        cell( ... )
```

```
DEF dead = 0,  alive = NOT dead :          -- possible states of each cell


DEF radius    = 1 ,              -- radius of the 'sphere of influence'
    diameter  = (2 * radius) + 1 ,
    neighbours = (diameter * diameter) - 1 :
                                -- consequent number of neighbours



PROC calculate.next.state(CHAN link[],
                          VALUE in[], state, VAR next.state) =
  VAR count :   -- number of living neighbours
  SEQ
    VAR state.of.neighbour[neighbours] :
    SEQ
      PAR i = [0 FOR neighbours]              -- receive present state
        link[in[i]] ? state.of.neighbour[i]  --    from each neighbour
      count := 0
      SEQ i = [0 FOR neighbours]
        IF
          state.of.neighbour[i] = alive
            count := count + 1                -- count the number alive
          state.of.neighbour[i] = dead
            SKIP
    IF
      count < 2                  -- if too few
        next.state := dead       --    die from isolation
      count = 2                  -- if exactly two
        next.state := state      --    this cell is stable
      count = 3                  -- if exactly three
        next.state := alive      --    give birth if dead
      count > 3                  -- if too many
        next.state := dead  :    --    die from overcrowding



PROC broadcast.present.state(CHAN link[], VALUE out[], state) =
  -- satisfy each neighbour's need to know this cell's state
  PAR i = [0 FOR neighbours]
    link[out[i]] ! state                     :
```

```
DEF set.state = 1, ask.state = 2, terminate = 3 :


PROC cell(CHAN link[], VALUE in[], out[], CHAN control, sense) =
  -- calculate the state of a single cell on the board
  VAR state, instruction :
  SEQ
    state := dead                  -- the whole board starts off dead
    control ? instruction
    WHILE instruction <> terminate
      SEQ
        IF                         -- on instruction
          instruction = set.state
            control ? state        --      accept a new state
          instruction = ask.state
            VAR next.state :
            SEQ                     --      or calculate the next state
              PAR
                broadcast.present.state(link, out, state)
                SEQ
                  calculate.next.state(link, in, state, next.state)
                  sense ! (state <> next.state); next.state
                                   --      announce it to the controller
              state := next.state  --      and move on a generation
        control ? instruction                              :
```

```
DEF array.width = 50,
    array.height = 20 :

DEF number.of.cells = array.height * array.width ,
    number.of.links = neighbours * number.of.cells :

PROC initialize(VALUE x, y, VAR in[], out[]) =
  -- initialize the link indirection arrays for the cell at x,y
  SEQ delta.x = [-radius FOR diameter]          -- offset of neighbour
    SEQ delta.y = [-radius FOR diameter]        -- in two dimensions
      VAR direction :   -- -4 <= direction <= +4
      SEQ
        direction := delta.x + (diameter * delta.y)
        IF
          direction <> 0
            VAR index, process :
            SEQ
              -- select outgoing channel in this direction
              process := x + (array.width * y)
              index   := (neighbours + direction) \ (neighbours + 1)
              out[index] := index + (neighbours * process)
              -- and select the corresponding incoming channel
              process := ((x + delta.x + array.width) \ array.width) +
                  (array.width *
                          ((y + delta.y + array.height) \ array.height))
              index   := (neighbours - direction) \ (neighbours + 1)
              in[index] := index + (neighbours * process)

          direction = 0        -- this cell is not its own neighbour
            SKIP                                          :
```

```
DEF control = NOT ((NOT 0) << 5),  escape = control /\ '[' :


PROC move.cursor(CHAN screen, VALUE x, y) =
  -- move to column x of line y (of a VT52)
  screen ! escape; 'Y'; '*s' + y; '*s' + x :

PROC clear.screen(CHAN screen) =
  -- clear the screen (of a VT52)
  screen ! escape; 'H' ; escape ; 'J' :


PROC initialize.display(CHAN screen) =
  -- display an entirely dead board
  clear.screen(screen)  :

PROC clean.up.display(CHAN screen) =
  -- move away from board
  move.cursor(screen, 0, array.height)  :

PROC display.state(CHAN screen, VALUE x, y, state) =
  -- display the state of one cell
  SEQ
    move.cursor(screen, x, y)
    IF
      state = alive          -- live cells show as an asterisk
        screen ! '**'
      state = dead           -- dead ones as a blank space
        screen ! '*s'                        :


PROC generation(CHAN screen, control[], sense[], VAR active) =
  -- cause the colony on the board to move on one generation
  SEQ
    SEQ cell = [0 FOR number.of.cells]      -- invite each cell
      control[cell] ! ask.state             --     to make progress
    active := FALSE
    SEQ cell = [0 FOR number.of.cells]      -- for each cell
      VAR changed, next.state :
      SEQ
        sense[cell] ? changed; next.state   --     receive its new state
        IF
          changed                           --     and display it
            SEQ
              display.state(screen, cell \ array.width,
                                    cell / array.width, next.state)
              active := TRUE
          NOT changed
            SKIP                      :
```

```
PROC edit(CHAN keyboard, screen, control[]) =
  -- modify the colony on the board

  DEF ctrl = NOT ((NOT 0) << 5),  otherwise = TRUE :
  DEF left.key  = ctrl /\ 'H',    right.key = ctrl /\ 'L',
      up.key    = ctrl /\ 'K',    down.key  = ctrl /\ 'J',
      uproot.key = '*s',          plant.key = '**' :

  VAR x, y, editing, ch :
  SEQ
    x := array.width / 2       -- set co-ordinates of cursor
    y := array.height / 2      -- to the centre of the board
    editing := TRUE
    WHILE editing
      SEQ
        move.cursor(screen, x, y)
        keyboard ? ch
        IF
          (ch = left.key) AND (x > 0)
            x := x - 1
          (ch = right.key) AND (x < (array.width - 1))
            x := x + 1
          (ch = up.key) AND (y > 0)
            y := y - 1
          (ch = down.key) AND (y < (array.height - 1))
            y := y + 1
          (ch = uproot.key) OR            -- change the state of the
                    (ch = plant.key)      -- cell under the cursor
            VAR state :
            SEQ
              state := (dead /\ (ch = uproot.key)) \/
                       (alive /\ (ch = plant.key))
              control[x + (array.width * y)] ! set.state; state
              display.state(screen, x, y, state)
          (ch = 'q') OR (ch = 'Q')
            editing := FALSE
          otherwise -- ignore anything that is not understood
            SKIP                                    :
```

```
DEF idle            = 1,
    editing         = 2,
    single.stepping = 3,
    free.running    = 4,
    terminated      = 5 :

PROC display.activity(CHAN screen, VALUE activity) =
  -- display state of the controller
  SEQ
    move.cursor(screen, array.width + 1, array.height / 2)
        -- move to a place off the right of the board
    IF
      activity = idle
        write.string(screen, "Idle")
      activity = editing
        write.string(screen, "Edit")
      activity = single.stepping
        write.string(screen, "Step")
      activity = free.running
        write.string(screen, "Busy")
      activity = terminated
        write.string(screen, "Done")


PROC new.activity(VAR activity, VALUE ch) =
  IF                             -- type 'ch' on the keyboard ...
    (ch = 'q') OR (ch = 'Q')     -- ... Q to finish the program
      activity := terminated
    (ch = 's') OR (ch = 'S')     -- ... S to halt evolution
      activity := idle
    (ch = 'e') OR (ch = 'E')     -- ... E to start editing
      activity := editing
    (ch = 'r') OR (ch = 'R')     -- ... R to start evolution
      activity := free.running
    otherwise                    -- ... or anything else for
                                 --     just one generation
      activity := single.stepping :
```

```
PROC controller(CHAN keyboard, screen, control[], sense[]) =
  -- control the activity of the colony on the board
  -- under direction from the keyboard
  VAR activity :
  SEQ
    activity := idle
    initialize.display(screen)
    WHILE activity <> terminated
      SEQ
        display.activity(screen, activity)
        VAR ch :
        PRI ALT
          (activity <> editing) & keyboard ? ch
                 -- if not editing, type to change activity
            new.activity(activity, ch)
          (activity = editing) & SKIP
            SEQ
              edit(keyboard, screen, control)
              activity := idle
          (activity = free.running) OR       -- if evolving
          (activity = single.stepping) &
                   SKIP                       -- but nothing typed
            VAR changing :
            SEQ
              generation(screen, control, sense, changing)
                                        -- move on a generation
              IF
                (activity = single.stepping) OR (NOT changing)
                  activity := idle
                (activity = free.running) AND changing
                  SKIP
      display.activity(screen, activity)
      SEQ cell = [0 FOR number.of.cells]
        control[cell] ! terminate
      clean.up.display(screen)                         :


CHAN link[number.of.links],
     control[number.of.cells],
     sense[number.of.cells] :
PAR
  controller(keyboard, screen, control, sense)    -- control process
  PAR x = [0 FOR array.width]                      -- board
    PAR y = [0 FOR array.height]
      VAR in[neighbours], out[neighbours] :
      SEQ
        initialize(x, y, in, out)
        cell(link, in, out,
             control[x+(array.width*y)], sense[x+(array.width*y)])
```

Simple Huffman coder

```
PROC insert.new.node( VAR new.node, VALUE weight.of.new.node,
                      VAR left.limit, VALUE right.limit       )

PROC construct.tree(VALUE probability[])

  PROC construct.leaves
    -- build the leaves of the tree

  PROC construct.other.nodes
    -- join pairs of subtrees until only one tree remains

  PROC invert.representation
    -- set parent[] and representative[]

  -- construct.tree

PROC encode.character(CHAN output, VALUE ch)
  -- Transmit the encoding of ch along output

PROC decode.character(CHAN input, VAR ch)

PROC copy.encoding(CHAN source, end.of.source, sink)
  -- Read characters from source, sending their encodings along
  -- sink, until a signal is received along end.of.source.

PROC copy.decoding(CHAN source, sink)
  -- Read a bit stream from source, decoding it into characters
  -- and send these along sink until end.of.message is decoded
```

```
DEF bits.in.character    = 8,
    number.of.characters = 1 << bits.in.character,
    number.of.codes      = number.of.characters,
    character.mask       = NOT ((NOT 0) << bits.in.character) :



DEF root = 0,  size.of.tree = (2 * number.of.codes) - 1 :



VAR  eldest[size.of.tree],
     parent[size.of.tree],
     character[size.of.tree],
     representative[number.of.characters] :



PROC insert.new.node( VAR new.node, VALUE weight.of.new.node,
                      VAR left.limit, VALUE right.limit        ) =
  VAR weight.limit :
  SEQ
    IF
      IF node = [left.limit FOR right.limit - left.limit]
        weight[node] <= weight.of.new.node
          weight.limit := node
      TRUE
        weight.limit := right.limit
    SEQ node = [left.limit FOR weight.limit - left.limit]
      SEQ
        character[node - 1] := character[node]
        eldest[node - 1]    := eldest[node]
        weight[node - 1]    := weight[node]
    left.limit := left.limit - 1
    new.node := weight.limit - 1
    weight[new.node] := weight.of.new.node                    :
```

```
PROC construct.tree(VALUE probability[]) =
  VAR left.limit, right.limit, weight[size.of.tree] :

  PROC construct.leaves =
    -- build the leaves of the tree
    DEF minimum.character = - (number.of.characters / 2) :
    SEQ ch = [minimum.character FOR number.of.characters]
      VAR new.node :
      SEQ
        insert.new.node(new.node, probability[ch /\ character.mask],
                                            left.limit, right.limit)
        eldest[new.node]    := root
        character[new.node] := ch            :

  PROC construct.other.nodes =
    -- join pairs of subtrees until only one tree remains
    WHILE (right.limit - left.limit) <> 1
      VAR new.node :
        SEQ
          right.limit := right.limit - 2
          insert.new.node(new.node,
                          weight[right.limit] + weight[right.limit+1],
                                            left.limit, right.limit)
          eldest[new.node] := right            :

  PROC invert.representation =
    -- set parent[] and representative[]
    SEQ node = [root FOR size.of.tree]
      IF
        eldest[node] = root
        representative[character[node] /\ character.mask] := node
        eldest[node] <> root
          SEQ child = [eldest[node] FOR 2]
            parent[child] := node                                :

SEQ
  left.limit   := size.of.tree + 1
  right.limit  := size.of.tree + 1
  -- here  left.limit = (size.of.tree + 1)
  -- and   (right.limit - left.limit) = 0
  construct.leaves
  -- here  left.limit = number.of.code
  -- and   (right.limit - left.limit) = number.of.codes
  construct.other.nodes
  -- here  left.limit = root
  -- and   (right.limit - left.limit) = 1
  invert.representation                        :
```

```
PROC encode.character(CHAN output, VALUE ch) =
  -- Transmit the encoding of ch along output
  DEF size.of.encoding = number.of.codes - 1 :
  VAR encoding[size.of.encoding], length, node :
  SEQ
    length := 0
    node   := representative[ch /\ character.mask]
    WHILE node <> root
      SEQ
        encoding[length] := node - eldest[parent[node]]
        length := length + 1
        node   := parent[node]
    SEQ i = [1 FOR length]
      output ! encoding[length - i]                    :
```

```
PROC decode.character(CHAN input, VAR ch) =
  VAR node :
  SEQ
    node := root
    WHILE eldest[node] <> root
      VAR bit :
      SEQ
        input ? bit
        node := eldest[node] + bit
    ch := character[node]                    :
```

```
DEF probability = TABLE[ ... ] :
  -- indexed by [0 FOR number.of.characters]
```

```
DEF end.of.message = -1 :
```

```
PROC copy.encoding(CHAN source, end.of.source, sink) =
  -- Read characters from source, sending their encodings along
  -- sink, until a signal is received along end.of.source.
  VAR more.characters.expected :
  SEQ
    construct.tree(probability)
    more.characters.expected := TRUE
    WHILE more.characters.expected
      VAR ch :
      ALT
        source ? ch
          encode.character(sink, ch)
        end.of.source ? ANY
          more.characters.expected := FALSE
    encode.character(sink, end.of.message)                :


PROC copy.decoding(CHAN source, sink) =
  -- Read a bit stream from source, decoding it into characters
  -- and send these along sink until end.of.message is decoded
  VAR more.characters.expected :
  SEQ
    construct.tree(probability)
    more.characters.expected := TRUE
    WHILE more.characters.expected
      VAR ch :
      SEQ
        decode.character(source, ch)
        IF
          ch <> end.of.message
            sink ! ch
          ch = end.of.message
            more.characters.expected := FALSE    :
```

Adaptive Huffman coder

```
PROC construct.tree

PROC create.leaf(VAR new.leaf, VALUE ch)

PROC swap.trees(VALUE i, j)

  PROC swap.words(VAR p, q)

  PROC adjust.offspring(VALUE i)

PROC increment.frequency(VALUE ch)

PROC encode.character(CHAN output, VALUE ch)

PROC decode.character(CHAN input, VAR ch)

PROC copy.encoding(CHAN source, end.of.source, sink)

PROC copy.decoding(CHAN source, sink)
```

```
DEF bits.in.character     = 8,
    number.of.characters = 1 << bits.in.character,
    number.of.codes      = number.of.characters + 1,
    character.mask       = NOT ((NOT 0) << bits.in.character) :


DEF root        = 0,
    size.of.tree = (2 * number.of.codes) - 1,
    not.a.node  = size.of.tree, :


VAR  escape,
     weight[size.of.tree],
     eldest[size.of.tree],
     parent[size.of.tree],
     character[size.of.tree],
     representative[number.of.characters] :


PROC construct.tree =
  -- Create a tree for the encoding in which every character is escaped
  SEQ
    escape := root
    weight[escape] := 1
    eldest[escape] := root      -- it is a leaf
    SEQ ch = [0 FOR number.of.characters]
      representative[ch] := not.a.node                    :


PROC create.leaf(VAR new.leaf, VALUE ch) =
  -- Extend the tree by fision of the escape leaf into two new leaves
  VAR new.escape :
  SEQ
    new.leaf              := escape + 1
    new.escape            := escape + 2

    eldest[escape]        := new.leaf      -- escape is the new parent

    weight[new.leaf]      := 0
    eldest[new.leaf]      :=root
    parent[new.leaf]      := escape
    character[new.leaf]   := ch
    representative[ch /\ character.mask] := new.leaf

    weight[new.esape]     := 1
    eldest[new.escape]    := root
    parent[new.escape]    := escape

    escape                := new.escape               :
```

```
PROC swap.trees(VALUE i, j) =
  -- Exchange disjoint sub-trees rooted at i and j

  PROC swap.words(VAR p, q) =
    -- Exchange values stored in p and q
    VAR t :
    SEQ
      t := p
      p := q
      q := t                   :

  PROC adjust.offspring(VALUE i) =
    -- Restore downstream pointers to node i
    IF
      eldest[i] = root
        representative[character[i] /\ character.mask] := i
      eldest[i] <> root
        SEQ child = [eldest[i] FOR 2]
          parent[child] := i                              :

  SEQ
    swap.words(eldest[i], eldest[j])
    swap.words(character[i], character[j])
    adjust.offspring(i)
    adjust.offspring(j)                                   :
```

```
PROC increment.frequency(VALUE ch) =
  -- Adjust the weights of all relevant nodes to account for one more
  -- occurrence of ch, and adjust the shape of the tree if necessary
  VAR node :
  SEQ
    IF
      representative[ch /\ character.mask] <> not.a.node
        node := representative[ch /\ character.mask]
      representative[ch /\ character.mask] = not.a.node
        create.leaf(node, ch)
    WHILE node <> root
      IF
        weight[node-1] > weight[node]
          SEQ
            weight[node] := weight[node] + 1
            node := parent[node]
        weight[node-1] = weight[node]
          IF i = [1 FOR (node - root) - 1]
            weight[(node - i) - 1] > weight[node]
              SEQ
                swap.trees(node, node - i)
                node := node - i
    weight[root] := weight[root] + 1 :
```

```
PROC encode.character(CHAN output, VALUE ch) =
  -- Transmit the encoding of ch along output
  DEF size.of.encoding = bits.in.character + (number.of.codes - 1)  :
  VAR encoding[size.of.encoding], length, node :
  SEQ
    IF
      representative[ch /\ character.mask] <> not.a.node
        SEQ
          length := 0
          node   := representative[ch /\ character.mask]
      representative[ch /\ character.mask] <> not.a.node
        SEQ
          SEQ i = [0 FOR bits.in.character]
            encoding[i] := (ch >> i) /\ 1   -- i'th bit of unencoded ch
          length := bits.in.character
          node   := escape
    WHILE node <> root
      SEQ
        encoding[length] := node - eldest[parent[node]]
        length := length + 1
        node   := parent[node]
    SEQ i = [1 FOR length]
      output ! encoding[length - i]                    :
```

```
PROC decode.character(CHAN input, VAR ch) =
  -- Receive an encoding along input and
  -- store the corresponding character in ch
  VAR node :
  SEQ
    node := root
    WHILE eldest[node] <> root
      VAR bit :
      SEQ
        input ? bit
        node := eldest[node] + bit
    IF
      node < escape
        ch := character[node]
      node = escape
        VAR bit :
        SEQ
          input ? bit
          ch := - bit
          SEQ i = [2 FOR bits.in.character - 1]
            SEQ
              input ? bit
              ch := (ch << 1) \/ bit          :


DEF end.of.message = -1 :

PROC copy.encoding(CHAN source, end.of.source, sink) =
  -- Read a stream of characters from source, until signalled on
  -- end.of.source, and transmit their encodings in sequence along
  -- sink, followed by that of end.of.message, maintaining throughout
  -- the encoding tree for the encoding determined by the cumulative
  -- frequencies of the characters transmitted
  VAR more.characters.expected :
  SEQ
    construct.tree
    more.characters.expected := TRUE
    WHILE more.characters.expected
      VAR ch :
      ALT
        source ? ch
          SEQ
            encode.character(sink, ch)
            increment.frequency(ch)
        end.of.source ? ANY
          more.characters.expected := FALSE
    encode.character(sink, end.of.message)          :
```

```
PROC copy.decoding(CHAN source, sink) =
  -- Read the encodings of a stream of characters, up to and including
  -- the encoding of end.of.message, from source and transmit the
  -- corresponding characters along sink, maintaining the encoding tree
  -- for the encoding determined by the cumulative frequencies of the
  -- characters received
  VAR more.characters.expected :
  SEQ
    construct.tree
    more.characters.expected := TRUE
    WHILE more.characters.expected
      VAR ch :
      SEQ
        decode.character(source, ch)
        IF
          ch <> end.of.message
            SEQ
              sink ! ch
              increment.frequency(ch)
          ch = end.of.message
            more.characters.expected := FALSE :
```

Index